Alternative & Non-Prescription Medicines

CHRISTINA BUNCE
& ANNE FENNELL

Capella

This edition printed 2004

For: Bookmart Limited
Registered Number 2372865
Trading as Bookmart Limited
Blaby Road, Wigston, Leicester LE18 4SE

Revised edition of title published as '*Non-Prescription Medicines
and Alternative Remedies*'.

Cover design by Alex Ingr
Text design by Chris Smith

© Arcturus Publishing Limited, 2002
Unit 26/27 Bickels Yard, 151-153 Bermondsey Street
London SE1 3HA

ISBN 1-84193-257-4

Printed and bound in China

CONTENTS

INTRODUCTION   4

ALTERNATIVE REMEDIES   5 – 48

- *FOR THROAT AND LUNGS*   8
- *FOR HEAD AND NECK*   17
- *FOR STOMACH AND DIGESTIVE SYSTEM*   19
- *FOR EARS, EYES AND MOUTH*   25
- *FOR BLOOD AND CIRCULATORY SYSTEM*   27
- *FOR MENTAL HEALTH*   29
- *FOR FEMALE REPRODUCTIVE SYSTEM*   35
- *FOR SKIN*   36
- *FOR BONES AND MUSCLES*   42
- *FOR CHILDREN'S DISORDERS*   48

OVER-THE-COUNTER MEDICINES   49

INTRODUCTION

The range of medicines at our disposal has never been greater than it is today. We have access not only to the conventional pills and potions prescribed by doctors, but to a range of alternative, complementary and Over-the-Counter products which we can buy without a prior medical consultation. While this is undoubtedly a good thing, in that many people do not feel that conventional medicine meets their needs, it also means that the average consumer is faced with a bewildering array of options to choose from.

This book is designed as a guide to the most common complementary and conventional medicines; aiding your understanding of each medicine and the quantity to administer. It is divided into two sections:

ALTERNATIVE REMEDIES
A guide to homeopathic and herbal medicines organised by the type of conditions they are most commonly used to treat.

OVER-THE-COUNTER MEDICINES
An A-Z of many, but by no means all, of the most commonly used Over-the-Counter remedies for common complaints.

IMPORTANT
If a problem persists and does not respond to Over-the-Counter treatment or alternative therapy, you should consult a medical professional. This book is not intended as a substitute for professional medical advice.

ALTERNATIVE
REMEDIES

Alternative or complementary medicine is a designation for any medical system which is based on a theory other than that taught in traditional Western medical schools. The popularity of alternative medicine has grown dramatically over the last decade and it is estimated that 80 per cent of people in the UK have either taken a complementary remedy or consulted a complementary practitioner at some time or another.

The most widely used types of remedies are homeopathic and herbal, and for this reason we have focused on them in this section.

HOMEOPATHY

Homeopathy is a system of medicine which is based on the principle that that the substance which causes a medical problem can also be used to cure it. This is known as the 'like cures like' theory. The patient is treated with minute amounts of substances that are themselves capable of producing the symptoms of the problem in question. For example, the homeopathic remedy recommended to treat diarrhoea may be a very dilute laxative.

Homeopathic remedies derive from vegetable, animal and mineral substances which are diluted in water or alcohol. Critics say the substances are diluted to the point where they cannot be of any medical value. However, homeopaths argue that another principle of homeopathy is 'less is more', so the more dilute a preparation, the more powerful its action. Following the dilution process, the substance is shaken rapidly until the desired strength is achieved.

The dosage for homeopathic remedies relates to the amount of times the original substance has been diluted and shaken.
Three dosages are commonly available:
• 6x, which has been diluted in a 1 to 9 ratio with 6 repeats
of the shaking process
• 6c, which has been diluted in a 1 to 99 ratio with 6 repeats
of the shaking process
• 30c, which has been diluted in a 1 to 99 ratio with 30 repeats
of the shaking process

Many homeopathic remedies can be bought over the counter from chemists and health food shops, but the very strong preparations can only be prescribed by a registered homeopath who will take a holistic approach to treatment, bearing in mind the patient's personality as well as symptoms.

As with any type of medication, you should always read the label carefully before taking or administering any homeopathic remedy – the number of tablets you should take depends on a range of factors. The remedies should be dissolved on the tongue and taken when your mouth is as clean as possible. It is not advisable to ingest any other substance – especially tea, coffee or toothpaste – within 30 minutes of taking homeopathic remedies, as this may affect their action. Avoid touching the tablets with your hands. Women who are pregnant or breastfeeding should consult a doctor or pharmacist before embarking on treatment.

HERBAL MEDICINE
Herbal medicine is a system of treatment in which different plants are used in order to treat symptoms of illness and to promote health. Herbal medicine has been the most common form of medical treatment in many cultures for centuries.

Although some traditional herbalists claim that it is crucial for extracts of the whole plant to be used in order for the maximum benefit of herbs to be realised, modern herbal remedies are made from the leaves, bark, roots, flowers or oils of plants. They can be taken as tablets, drops that are added to water, or teas. Some are also available as creams or ointments.

Herbal remedies can now be bought from most pharmacies and healthfood shops. As with all kinds of medicine it is vital to read the instructions carefully before taking or administering any herbal remedy. They can be harmful if not taken appropriately and they can have unwanted side effects. Breastfeeding or pregnant women should not take any kind of remedy without prior consultation with a doctor or pharmacist. Many herbal remedies are not suitable for children.

SELF-TREATMENT WITH COMPLEMENTARY REMEDIES
There is a widely held belief that complementary medicines are always harmless. This is not the case. Some of the most potent and dangerous medicines used in orthodox medicine are derived from natural substances, for instance the heart drug digoxin is derived from the common foxglove.

It is important therefore to approach complementary medicine with the same caution as you would orthodox medication, and observe the following guidelines:

• Only attempt to treat minor ailments yourself – if in doubt, speak to a GP or pharmacist
• Ask for advice if you are not sure which is the most suitable preparation for your need
• Read the packet very carefully and take note of how much to take, when and how – if in doubt, ask an expert
• Be extra vigilant when treating children – particularly with the dosage
• Check the use-by date
• Seek advice first if you are pregnant or breastfeeding
• Do not take without seeking advice if you have been prescribed prescription medicines
• Keep away from children
• If symptoms do not improve, seek further advice.

HOW TO USE THIS SECTION

Included in this part of the book is a selection of many of the basic herbal and homeopathic remedies that are most widely available. The list is not exhaustive and you will find other brands of many of the substances. The organization in this section differs from the alphabetical arrangement adopted in the section for Over-the-Counter medicines. The entries are arranged firstly by the disorder for which treatment is being sought, then alphabetically by name. The name may be the title of a specific preparation (for example, bryonia) or the name of the product's originator or manufacturer (for example, Potter's or Weleda).

The disorders for which treatments are given are for those affecting:

• *Throat and lungs*
• *Head and neck*
• *Stomach and digestive system*
• *Ears, eyes and mouth*
• *Blood and circulatory system*
• *Mental health*
• *Female reproductive system*
• *The skin*
• *Bones and muscles*
• *Children*

REMEDIES FOR THROAT AND LUNG DISORDERS

ACONITE
What it is: A homeopathic remedy which should be taken during the early stages of a cold. Also suitable for sore throats, fevers or dry, persistent coughs.
Dose: Ainsworth's 30c, Nelsons 6c, Weleda 6c and 30c.

ALLIUM CEPA
What it is: A homeopathic remedy for the treatment of colds and catarrh. It can also be used for hayfever and laryngitis.
Dose: Ainsworth's 30c, Weleda 6c.

APIS MELLIFICA
What it is: A homeopathic remedy for relieving a sore and burning throat.
Dose: Weleda 6c and 30c, Nelsons 6c.

ARGENTUM NITRICUM
What it is: A homeopathic remedy for treating hoarseness and a sore throat.
Dose: Weleda 6c and 30c, Nelsons 6c, Ainsworth's 30c.

BELLADONNA
What it is: A homeopathic remedy for the treatment of sudden fevers.
Dose: Nelsons 6c, Weleda 6c and 30c.

BIO-STRATH CHAMOMILE FORMULA
What it is: A herbal liquid remedy which can be used to ease the symptoms of sore throats. It contains camomile, sage and yeast.
Dose: 20 drops should be diluted in water three times a day before meals. This treatment is not suitable for children.

BIO-STRATH THYME FORMULA
What it is: A liquid herbal cough remedy containing thyme, primula and yeast.
Dose: 20 drops should be taken in water three times a day before meals.

BRYONIA
What it is: A homeopathic remedy for the treatment of dry, irritating coughs.
Dose: Ainsworth's 30c, Nelsons 6c, Weleda 6c and 30c.

BUTTERCUP POL 'N' COUNT
What it is: A herbal remedy for relieving the symptoms of hayfever. It contains garlic and echinacea.

Dose: Two tablets should be taken three times a day. This treatment is not suitable for children.

CALCAREA FLUORICA
What it is: A homeopathic remedy for the treatment of coughs which are accompanied by yellow mucus.
Dose: Nelsons 6c, New Era 6x, Weleda 6c and 30c.

CALCAREA PHOSPHORICA
What it is: A homeopathic remedy for the treatment bronchial asthma and catarrh.
Dose: Nelsons 6c, New Era 6x, Weleda 6c and 30c.

CALCAREA SULPHURICA
What it is: A homeopathic remedy for the treatment of catarrh.
Dose: New Era 6x.

CARBO VEGETABILIS
What it is: A homeopathic remedy for relieving violent coughing.
Dose: Nelsons 6c, Weleda 6c and 30c.

CATARRH CREAM
What it is: An aromatic herbal decongestant which can be used to ease the congestion and inflamed nasal passages caused by catarrh. It contains camphor, eucalyptus, echinacea, thyme, barberry, blackthorn, bryonia, aesculin and mercurius sulphuratus.
Dose: A small amount of cream should be inserted into each nostril as required. It is not advisable to combine this treatment with homeopathic remedies. This treatment is not suitable for use on children under three years.

CATARRH-EEZE
What it is: A traditional herbal remedy used to relieve the congestion caused by catarrh. It contains inula, horehound and yarrow.
Dose: Adults should take two tablets three times a day. Children (8-12 years) should take one tablet three times a day.

COLD-EEZE
What it is: A tablet herbal remedy for relieving colds, containing garlic and echinacea.
Dose: Two tablets should be swallowed whole, three times a day. This treatment is not suitable for children.

COUGH EEZE
What it is: An expectorant herbal cough remedy available in the form of tablets. It contains ipecacuanha, inula and horehound.

Dose: Adults should take two tablets, three times a day. Children (8-12 years) should take one tablet a day.

DROSERA
What it is: A homeopathic remedy for the treatment of tickly, irritating coughs and violent coughing attacks. It is also useful for laryngitis and sore throats where swallowing is painful.
Dose: Ainsworth's 30c, Nelsons 6c, Weleda 6c and 30c.

ECHINACEA AND GARLIC
What it is: A herbal tablet remedy for the relief and treatment of colds and flu.
Dose: 1-2 tablets should be taken three times a day. This treatment is not suitable for children.

ERNEST JACKSON'S CATARRH PASTILLES
What it is: Herbal pastilles for the treatment of catarrh. They contain menthol, creosote, abietis pine oil and sylvestris pine oil.
Dose: Dissolve one pastille in the mouth when required.

ERNEST JACKSON'S CHILDREN'S COUGH PASTILLES
What it is: Expectorant herbal pastilles containing ipecacuanha, citric acid, honey, and squill.
Dose: One pastille should be dissolved in the mouth. Read the label for the maximum amount that can be taken in 24 hours.

EUPHRASIA
What it is: A homeopathic remedy for the treatment of daytime coughs which produce mucus.
Dose: Ainsworth's 30c, Nelsons 6c, Weleda 6c and 30c.

FERRUM PHOSPHORICUM
What it is: A homeopathic remedy to be used during the early stages of a cold or fever, after using aconite.
Dose: Ainsworth's 30c, Nelsons 6c, New Era 6x, Weleda 6c and 30c.

GARLODEX
What it is: A herbal tablet remedy for the treatment and relief of colds and catarrh, containing garlic, parsley and marshmallow.
Dose: One tablet should be taken three times a day. Children (5-12 years) should take one tablet at bedtime. This treatment is not suitable for children under five years.

GELSEMIUM
What it is: A homeopathic remedy for sore throats where swallowing is painful or difficult.
Dose: Weleda 6c and 30c, Nelsons 6c, Ainsworth's 30c.

GENCYDO
What it is: This is an ointment containing quince, lemon juice and boric acid and is used for relieving the symptoms of hayfever.
Dose: The ointment should be applied to the inside of the nostrils several times a day and before retiring. It is also available as a nasal paint that can be diluted with water and used as a nasal spray.

HEATH & HEATHER BALM OF GILEAD COUGH PASTILLES
What it is: Herbal expectorant cough pastilles for treating general coughs. They contain balm of Gilead, lobelia and squill.
Dose: One pastille should be dissolved in the mouth as required. Take a maximum of 12 pastilles over 24 hours.

HEATH & HEATHER CATARRH TABLETS
What it is: Herbal tablets which can be used to relieve the symptoms of catarrh. The tablets contain white horehound and squill.
Dose: One tablet should be taken three times a day. This treatment is not suitable for children.

HEPAR SULPHURIS
What it is: A homeopathic remedy for the treatment of coughs that are brought on by cold air.
Dose: Ainsworth's 30c, Nelsons 6c, Weleda 6c and 30c.

HERBELIX
What it is: A liquid herbal expectorant which can relieve the symptoms of catarrh. It contains lobelia, tolu solution and sodium bicarbonate.
Dose: 5 ml should be taken at bedtime. Children (7-14 years) should be given half the adult dose. This treatment is not suitable for children under seven years.

HOFELS GARLIC AND PARSLEY ONE-A DAY TABLETS
What it is: A herbal remedy for the relief of colds, catarrh and hayfever. The tablets contain garlic oil. This remedy is also available as Hofels Garlic One-A-Day Garlic Pearles, and Original Garlic Pearles.
Dose: One tablet should be taken with food. This treatment is not suitable for children under seven years.

IGNATIA
What it is: A homeopathic remedy for the treatment of dry, irritating

coughs and sore throats.
Dose: Nelsons 6c, Weleda 6c and 30c.

KALIUM BICHROMICUM
What it is: A homeopathic remedy for the treatment of stringy, persistent catarrh and sore throats.
Dose: Ainsworth's 30c, Nelsons 6c, Weleda 6c and 30c.

KALIUM MURIATICUM
What it is: A homeopathic remedy for the treatment of white, sticky catarrh and tonsillitis.
Dose: New Era 6x.

KALIUM PHOSPHORICUM
What it is: A homeopathic remedy for the treatment of asthma in cases where breathing is particularly difficult, or for nervous asthma accompanied by hoarseness.
Dose: Nelsons 6c, New Era 6x, Weleda 6c and 30c.

KALIUM SULPHURICUM
What it is: A homeopathic remedy for the treatment of asthma accompanied by bronchitis, and yellow catarrh.
Dose: New Era 6x.

LACHESIS
What it is: A homeopathic remedy for sore throats that extend to the ear and tonsillitis.
Dose: Weleda 6c.

LANES HONEY AND MOLASSES COUGH MIXTURE
What it is: A liquid herbal expectorant remedy containing ipecacuanha, horehound and squill.
Dose: Adults should take 5 ml three times a day. Children (2-14 years) should be given 2.5 ml. Read the label for the maximum dose.

LOBELIA COMPOUND
What it is: A herbal remedy available in the form of tablets that act as an anti-spasmodic, expectorant and respiratory stimulant. They contain lobelia, gum ammoniacum and squill.
Dose: One tablet should be taken three times a day.

LUSTY'S GARLIC PERLES
What it is: Herbal capsules for the treatment of colds, runny nose, catarrh and coughs. The capsules contain garlic.
Dose: One capsule should be taken three times a day with meals.

Children (5-12 years) should be given one capsule a day. This treatment is not suitable for children under five years.

MERCURIUS SOLUBILIS
What it is: A homeopathic remedy for relieving feverish head colds which are accompanied by catarrh.
Dose: Nelsons 6c, Weleda 6c and 30c.

NATRUM MURIATICUM
What it is: A homeopathic remedy for relieving the symptoms of hayfever.
Dose: Ainsworth's 30c, Nelsons 6c, New Era 6x, Weleda 6c and 30c.

NEW ERA COMBINATION H
What it is: A homeopathic remedy for relieving the symptoms of hayfever and allergic rhinitis. It contains mag phos, nat mur and silica.
Dose: One dose contains 6x each of the above ingredients.

NEW ERA COMBINATION Q
What it is: A homeopathic remedy for the treatment of catarrh and sinus disorders. It contains calc fluor, calc phos, kali phos and mag phos.
Dose: Each dose contains 6x each of the above ingredients.

NUX VOMICA
What it is: A homeopathic remedy which can be used to treat violent coughing fits and raw sore throats.
Dose: Ainsworth's 30c, Nelsons 6c, Weleda 6c and 30c.

OLBAS INHALER
What it is: An inhalant for relieving nasal congestion caused by colds and flu. It can also help to relieve congestion caused by catarrh, hayfever and blocked sinuses. It contains menthol, eucalyptus, peppermint and cajuput.
Dose: Place the inhaler in each nostril and inhale. Repeat up to four times in one hour. This treatment is not recommended for children under seven years.

OLBAS OIL
What it is: A liquid inhalation which can help to relieve nasal congestion caused by colds, flu, catarrh, hayfever, sinusitis and any infections of the upper respiratory tract. It contains menthol, eucalyptus, wintergreen, juniper berry, clove, mint and cajuput.
Dose: Put 2-3 drops on a handkerchief and inhale as required. The

liquid can be added to hot water and used as a steam inhalant. For children aged three months to two years, use one drop on a tissue and tie out of reach on clothing or bedhead at night. This treatment is not suitable for babies under three months.

OLBAS PASTILLES
What it is: Pastilles for the relief of cold and flu symptoms, containing menthol, eucalyptus, wintergreen, juniper berry, peppermint and cloves.
Dose: One pastille should be dissolved in the mouth as required. Take a maximum of eight pastilles over 24 hours. This treatment is not suitable for children under seven years.

OLEUM RHINALE
What it is: A herbal oil remedy which can help to relieve the symptoms of sinus congestion, dry rhinitis and catarrh. It contains eucalyptus, peppermint, marigold and mercurius sulphuratus.
Dose: 2-4 drops should be applied into each nostril twice a day. This treatment should not be combined with any other herbal or homeopathic remedies.

PHOSPHORUS
What it is: A homeopathic remedy for the treatment of a cough which causes breathing difficulties, laryngitis and hoarseness.
Dose: Ainsworth's 30c, Nelsons 6c, Weleda 6c and 30c.

PHYTOLACCA
What it is: A homeopathic remedy for the treatment of dry sore throats.
Dose: Weleda 6c.

POLLENNA
What it is: A homeopathic remedy for the treatment of hayfever, containing 6c each of Allium cepa, Euphrasia officinallis and Sabadilla officinarum.
Dose: Adults should take two tablets every two hours for six doses, then two tablets three times a day. Children should be given half the adult dose. Stop the treatment when symptoms cease.

POTTER'S ANTIBRON
What it is: A herbal tablet remedy that can be used as an anti-spasm, expectorant, soothing and sedative cough treatment. It contains lobelia, euphorbia, coltsfoot, pleurisy root, senega and wild lettuce.
Dose: Adults should take two tablets three times a day. Children over seven years should take one tablet as directed.

POTTER'S ANTISMOKING TABLETS

What it is: A herbal remedy for reducing nicotine dependence. The tablets contain lobelia.

Dose: One tablet should be taken every hour. Take a maximum of 10 tablets over 24 hours.

POTTER'S BALM OF GILEAD

What it is: A liquid herbal expectorant for the treatment of general coughs. It contains balm of Gilead, lobelia, lungwort and squill.

Dose: Adults should take 10 ml diluted in water 3-4 times a day. Children over five years should take 5 ml.

POTTER'S CATARRH MIXTURE

What it is: A liquid herbal remedy used to relieve nasal and throat catarrh. It contains capsicum, burdock, boneset, hyssop and blue flag.

Dose: Adults should take 5 ml three times a day. Children over seven years should be given 5 ml twice a day. This treatment is not suitable for children under seven years.

POTTER'S CHEST MIXTURE

What it is: An expectorant liquid herbal cough and catarrh remedy, containing lobelia, horehound, pleurisy root, senega and squill.

Dose: Adults should take 5 ml every three hours. This treatment is not suitable for children.

POTTER'S ELDERMINT LIFE DROPS

What it is: A homeopathic liquid remedy for the treatment of colds, flu, fevers and sore throats. It contains capsicum, elderflower and peppermint.

Dose: Adults should take 11 drops diluted in warm water every hour. Children over seven years should be given 11 drops every two hours. This treatment is not suitable for children under seven years. Do not combine this treatment with other homeopathic remedies.

POTTER'S GARLIC TABLETS

What it is: A herbal tablet remedy for the treatment of colds and flu, containing garlic.

Dose: Adults should take two tablets three times a day. Children over eight years should be given one tablet 3-4 times a day.

POTTER'S LIGHTNING COUGH REMEDY

What it is: A liquid herbal cough remedy containing liquorice and anise.

Dose: Adults should take 10 ml 3-4 times a day. Children over five years should be given 5 ml every 5-6 hours.

POTTER'S VEGETABLE COUGH REMOVER
What it is: A herbal liquid remedy that is an expectorant and an anti-spasmodic for relieving cough symptoms. It contains ipecacuanha, lobelia, hyssop, horehound, elecampane, black cohosh, pleurisy root and skullcap.
Dose: Adults, 10ml 3-4 times a day. Children over eight years, 5 ml three times a day. Children (5-7 years) 5 ml twice a day.

PULSATILLA
What it is: A homeopathic remedy for the treatment of thick, yellow catarrh.
Dose: Ainsworth's 30c, Nelsons 6c, Weleda 6c and 30c.

RESOLUTION
What it is: Lozenges for reducing nicotine dependence. They contain the vitamins A, C, E and nicotine.
Dose: One lozenge should be dissolved in the mouth when the urge to smoke a cigarette arises.

SILICA
What it is: A homeopathic remedy for relieving the symptoms of persistent colds and hayfever.
Dose: Ainsworth's 30c, Nelsons 6c, New Era 6x, Weleda 6c and 30c.

SINOTAR
What it is: A herbal tablet remedy that is an antiseptic and decongestant for relieving the symptoms of catarrh and sinusitis. It contains echinacea, marshmallow and elderflower.
Dose: Two tablets should be taken three times a day before meals. Children (5-12 years) should be given half the adult dose. This treatment is not suitable for children under five years.

STOPPERS
What it is: Lozenges containing nicotine for reducing nicotine dependence.
Dose: One lozenge should be dissolved in the mouth when the urge to smoke a cigarette arises.

THUJA
What it is: A homeopathic remedy for relieving catarrh.
Dose: Nelsons 6c, Weleda 6c and 30c.

WELEDA COUGH DROPS
What it is: A liquid herbal remedy containing aqua cherry laurel, angelica, cinnamon, coriander, clove, nutmeg, lemon balm and lemon oil.

Dose: 10-20 drops should be dissolved in warm water and swallowed every two hours.

WELEDA HERB AND HONEY COUGH ELIXIR
What it is: A liquid herbal cough remedy containing thyme, horehound, elderflower, Iceland moss, marshmallow and aniseed.
Dose: Adults should take 10 ml diluted in water every 3-4 hours. Take a maximum of four doses over 24 hours. Children over six years should be given half the adult dose.

WELEDA MIXED POLLEN
What it is: A homeopathic remedy for relieving the symptoms of hayfever. It contains a wide range of pollens.
Dose: 30c.

REMEDIES FOR HEAD AND NECK DISORDERS

ACTAEA RACEMOSA
What it is: A homeopathic remedy used for the treatment of headaches that begin with severe pain at the back of the head and tend to spread upwards.
Dose: Nelsons 6c, Weleda 6c.

BELLADONNA
What it is: A homeopathic remedy for relieving severe throbbing headaches.
Dose: Ainsworth's 30c, Nelsons 6c, Weleda 6c.

BRYONIA
What it is: A homeopathic remedy for relieving splitting headaches that occur over the eyes.
Dose: 30c, one tablet every four hours for a maximum of six doses.

CALCAREA PHOSPHORICA
What it is: A homeopathic remedy for relieving headaches caused by long periods of study.
Dose: Nelsons 6c, New Era 6x, Weleda 6c.

COFFEA
What it is: A homeopathic remedy for relieving nervous headaches occurring on one side of the head.
Dose: Weleda 6c.

FEVERFEW
What it is: A homeopathic remedy which can be used to reduce the severity and frequency of migraine headaches.
Dose: Weleda 6x.

GELSEMIUM
What it is: A homeopathic remedy for the treatment of general headaches, it is especially effective for those brought on by colds and flu.
Dose: Ainsworth's 30c, Nelsons 6c, Weleda 6c.

GLONOINE
What it is: A homeopathic remedy that can be used to treat thumping headaches.
Dose: One tablet every 30 minutes until an improvement occurs, for a maximum of six doses.

IGNATIA
What it is: A homeopathic remedy for relieving sharp, painful headaches.
Dose: Nelsons 6c, Weleda 6c or 30c.

KALIUM BICHROMICUM
What it is: A homeopathic remedy for relieving migraines which are preceded by blurred vision.
Dose: Nelsons 6c, Weleda 6c and 30c.

KALIUM PHOSPHORICUM
What it is: A homeopathic remedy for the treatment of stress-related headaches.
Dose: Nelsons 6c, New Era 6x, Weleda 6c.

LACHESIS
What it is: A homeopathic remedy for relieving throbbing headaches.
Dose: Weleda 6c.

NATRUM MURIATICUM
What it is: A homeopathic remedy for relieving severe headaches.
Dose: Ainsworth's 30c, Nelsons 6c, New Era 6x, Weleda 6c and 30c.

NEW ERA COMBINATION F
What it is: A combination of kali phos, mag phos, nat mur and silica for the treatment of migraine headaches.
Dose: One tablet containing 6x of each of the above ingredients.

NUX VOMICA
What it is: A homeopathic remedy for headaches which are accompanied by dizziness, nausea and sickness.
Dose: Nelsons 6c, Weleda 6c and 30c.

SILICA
What it is: A homeopathic remedy for the relief and treatment of migraine.
Dose: Ainsworth's 30c, Nelsons 6c, New Era 6x, Weleda 6c and 30c.

THUJA
What it is: A homeopathic remedy for severe headaches or migraine.
Dose: Nelsons 6c, Weleda 6c.

REMEDIES FOR DISORDERS AFFECTING THE STOMACH AND DIGESTIVE SYSTEM

ARGENTIUM NITRICUM
What it is: A homeopathic remedy for the treatment of nervous diarrhoea and heartburn.
Dose: Weleda 6c and 30c, Nelsons 6c, Ainsworth's 30c.

ARSENICUM ALBUM
What it is: A homeopathic remedy for the treatment of sudden diarrhoea with vomiting.
Dose: Weleda 6c and 30c, Nelsons 6c, Ainsworth's 30c.

BIOBALM POWDER
What it is: A herbal powder remedy for relieving indigestion, containing slippery elm, camomile, Irish moss and marshmallow.
Dose: 1-2 level teaspoons should be mixed with water and taken up to four times a day. Children (5-12 years) should be given half the adult dose. This treatment is not suitable for children under five years.

BIO-STRATH ARTICHOKE FORMULA
What it is: A herbal liquid remedy for relieving indigestion particularly after eating fatty foods.
Dose: Take two drops diluted in water three times a day before meals This treatment is not suitable for children and should not be combined with other homeopathic remedies.

BIO-STRATH LIQUORICE FORMULA
What it is: A herbal liquid remedy for aiding digestion. It contains

liquorice, camomile, gentian and yeast.
Dose: Take 2 ml diluted in water three times a day. This treatment is not suitable for children.

CALCAREA CARBONICA
What it is: A homeopathic remedy for relieving constipation, containing senna and aloes.
Dose: Nelsons 6c, Weleda 6c and 30c. This treatment is not suitable for children under seven years.

CARBO VEGETABILIS
What it is: A homeopathic remedy for treating indigestion with flatulence.
Dose: Weleda 6c and 30c, Nelsons 6c, Ainsworth's 30c.

CATASSIUM HERBAL TRAVEL SICKNESS TABLETS
What it is: A herbal tablet remedy for relieving travel sickness, containing ginger.
Dose: Adults should take three tablets 30 minutes before starting a journey. Children (6-12 years) should be given 1-2 tablets. This treatment is not suitable for children under six years.

CAUSTICUM
What it is: A homeopathic remedy to help relieve constipation where there is ineffectual urging.
Dose: Weleda 6c.

CLAIRO TEA
What it is: A herbal tea for relieving constipation. It contains senna (a stimulant laxative), aniseed, peppermint and clove.
Dose: Adults should take 2.5 ml dissolved in boiling water at night. Children over six years should be given half the adult dose in the morning. This treatment is not suitable for children under six years.

COCCULUS
What it is: A homeopathic remedy for relieving travel sickness and jetlag.
Dose: Weleda 6c, Ainsworth's 30c.

COLOCYNTHIS
What it is: A homeopathic remedy for relieving diarrhoea that is accompanied by abdominal cramps and spasms.
Dose: Weleda 6c.

CRANESBILL
What it is: A herbal tablet that provides astringent relief for non-persistent diarrhoea. It contains cranesbill.

Dose: 1-2 tablets should be taken as required, up to three times a day. Children over 12 years should take one tablet twice a day. This treatment is not suitable for children under 12 years.

DIGEST
What it is: A herbal tablet remedy for relieving indigestion and wind. It contains centaury, parsley and marshmallow.
Dose: Two tablets should be taken three times a day before meals. This treatment is not suitable for children under 12 years.

DUAL-LAX
What it is: A herbal tablet remedy for relieving constipation. The tablets contain senna and aloes, both of which are stimulant laxatives.
Dose: Adults should take 1-2 tablets at night. Children (7-14 years) should be given one tablet at night. This treatment is not suitable for children under seven years. An extra strength version is also available.

GINGER TABLETS
What it is: A herbal tablet remedy for calming nauseous sensations.
Dose: Take one tablet three times a day. This treatment is not suitable for children.

GLADLAX
What it is: A herbal tablet remedy for relieving constipation. It contains senna and aloes, both of which are stimulant laxatives.
Dose: Adults should take 1-2 tablets at night. Children (7-14 years) should be given one tablet at night. This treatment is not suitable for children under seven years.

GOLDEN SEAL COMPOUND
What it is: A herbal tablet remedy which can help to soothe and relieve nausea, containing golden seal, cranesbill, marshmallow root and dandelion.
Dose: Two tablets should be taken three times a day between meals. This treatment is not suitable for children under 12 years.

GRAPHITES
What it is: A homeopathic remedy for relieving constipation.
Dose: Weleda 6c and 30c, Nelsons 6c.

HERBULAX
What it is: A herbal tablet remedy for relieving constipation, containing dandelion and frangula.
Dose: Adults should take 1-2 tablets at bedtime. Children (5-12 years) should be given half to one tablet at bedtime. This treatment is not suitable for children under five years.

IGNATIA
What it is: A homeopathic remedy for relieving constipation.
Dose: Weleda 6c and 30c, Nelsons 6c.

INDIAN BRANDEE
What it is: A liquid mixture for relieving digestive discomfort, containing ginger, rhubarb and capsicum.
Dose: 5 ml should be taken in or with water, once or twice daily as required. This treatment is not suitable for children.

IPECACUANHA
What it is: A homeopathic remedy for relieving nausea and travel sickness.
Dose: Weleda 6c and 30c, Nelsons 6c.

KALIUM MURIATICUM
What it is: A homeopathic remedy for relieving indigestion caused by fatty foods.
Dose: New Era 6x.

LUSTY'S HERBALENE
What it is: A herbal mixture for relieving constipation, containing senna, fennel, frangula and elder.
Dose: 2.5 ml should be taken twice a day. The dose should be placed on the tongue and swallowed with water. This treatment is not suitable for children under seven years.

MELISSA COMPOUND
What it is: A herbal liquid remedy for relieving occasional diarrhoea, containing alcohol, archangelica, cinnamon, cloves, coriander, lemon, lemon balm and nutmeg.
Dose: 10-20 drops should be diluted in a little water, as required, up to eight times a day. Children over eight years should take 5-10 drops up to eight times a day. This treatment is not suitable for children under eight years. Do not combine with other homeopathic remedies without seeking advice first.

MERCURIUS SOLUBILIS
What it is: A homeopathic remedy for relieving diarrhoea with straining.
Dose: Weleda 6c and 30c, Nelsons 6c, Ainsworth's 30c.

NATRALEZE
What it is: A herbal tablet remedy for heartburn, indigestion and wind. It contains slippery elm, liquorice and meadowsweet.
Dose: 2.5-15 ml should be taken three times a day, according to age.

This treatment is not suitable for children under seven years.

NATRUM MURIATICUM
What it is: A homeopathic remedy to relieve constipation.
Dose: Weleda 6c and 30c, Nelsons 6c, New Era 6x, Ainsworth's 30c.

NATRUM PHOSPHORICUM
What it is: A homeopathic remedy for relieving indigestion.
Dose: New Era 6x.

NATRUM SULPHURICUM
What it is: A homeopathic remedy for relieving yellow diarrhoea.
Dose: New Era 6x.

NELSONS TRAVELLA
What it is: A homeopathic remedy for relieving travel sickness.
Dose: Adults should take two tablets every hour for two hours before starting on a journey, followed by two tablets every hour during the journey. Children should take half the adult dose.

NEW ERA COMBINATION C
What it is: A homeopathic remedy for relieving indigestion and heartburn. Contains mag phos, nat phos, nat sulp and silica.
Dose: One dose contains 6x of each of the above ingredients.

NEW ERA COMBINATION E
What it is: A homeopathic remedy for relieving indigestion, containing a combination of calc phos, mag phos, nat phos and nat sulph.
Dose: One dose contains 6x of each of the above ingredients.

NUX VOMICA
What it is: A homeopathic remedy for relieving constipation where there is ineffectual urging.
Dose: Weleda 6c and 30c, Nelsons 6c, New Era 6x, Ainsworth's 30c.

PAPAYA PLUS
What it is: A herbal tablet remedy for relieving heartburn, indigestion and wind. It contains papain, slippery elm, golden seal and charcoal.
Dose: One tablet should be taken before meals three times a day. This treatment is not suitable for children.

PILEWORT COMPOUND
What it is: A herbal tablet remedy for relieving constipation and piles, containing senna, cascara, cranesbill and pilewort.

Dose: 1-2 tablets should be taken at night. This treatment is not suitable for children under 12 years.

POTTER'S CLEANSING HERB
What it is: A herbal tablet remedy for relieving occasional constipation, containing fennel, valerian, aloes and holly thistle.
Dose: 1-2 tablets should be taken at bedtime. This product should not be taken during the day, as valerian has a sedative effect. This treatment is not suitable for children under 12 years.

POTTER'S CLEANSING HERB TABLETS
What it is: A herbal tablet remedy for relieving constipation, containing senna, cascara, aloes, fennel and dandelion.
Dose: 1-2 tablets should be taken at bedtime. This treatment is not suitable for children.

POTTER'S INDIGESTION MIXTURE
What it is: A herbal liquid remedy for relieving indigestion, heartburn and wind, containing meadowsweet, gentian and wahoo.
Dose: 5 ml should be taken 3-4 times a day after meals. This treatment is not suitable for children.

POTTER'S LION CLEANSING HERBAL TABLETS
What it is: A herbal tablet remedy for relieving constipation, containing cascara, aloes, fennel and dandelion.
Dose: 1-2 tablets should be taken at bedtime. This treatment is not suitable for children.

POTTER'S OUT OF SORTS TABLETS
What it is: A herbal tablet remedy for relieving constipation, containing senna, cascara, aloes fennel and dandelion.
Dose: 1-2 tablets should be taken at bedtime. This treatment is not suitable for children.

POTTER'S SLIPPERY ELM TABLETS
What it is: A herbal tablet remedy for relieving indigestion, heartburn and wind, containing slippery elm, peppermint, cinnamon and cloves.
Dose: 5 ml should be taken 3-4 times a day after meals. This treatment is not suitable for children.

POTTER'S SPANISH TUMMY MIXTURE
What it is: A herbal astringent mixture which can be used to relieve non-persistent diarrhoea, containing blackberry root and catechu.
Dose: 5 ml should be taken every hour, as required. This treatment is not suitable for children.

RHUAKA HERBAL SYRUP
What it is: A herbal syrup for relieving constipation, containing rhubarb, senna and cascara.
Dose: Adults should take 20 ml at bedtime. Children over seven years should be given 5 ml at bedtime. This treatment is not suitable for children under seven years.

SILICA
What it is: A homeopathic remedy for relieving constipation.
Dose: Weleda 6c and 30c, Nelsons 6c, New Era 6x, Ainsworth's 30c.

SULPHUR
What it is: A homeopathic remedy for relieving early morning diarrhoea.
Dose: Nelsons 6c, New Era 6c and 30c, Ainsworth's 30c.

REMEDIES FOR DISORDERS AFFECTING EARS, EYES AND MOUTH

ACONITE
What it is: A homeopathic remedy for relieving earaches which occur after exposure to cold, dry wind.
Dose: Weleda 6c and 30c, Nelsons 6c, Ainsworth's 30c.

ARGENTUM NITRICUM
What it is: A homeopathic remedy for earaches which cause buzzing in the ears.
Dose: Weleda 6c and 30c, Nelsons 6c, Ainsworth's 30c.

BELLADONNA
What it is: A homeopathic remedy for relieving throbbing earaches.
Dose: Weleda 6c and 30c, Nelsons 6c, Ainsworth's 30c.

CALCAREA SULPHURICA
What it is: A homeopathic remedy for treating abscesses which have begun to emit a discharge.
Dose: New Era 6x.

CHAMOMILLA
What it is: A homeopathic remedy which can be used for children's earaches. It can also be used for toothaches that worsen after taking a warm drink.
Dose: Weleda 3x and 30c, Ainsworth's 30c.

COFFEA
What it is: A homeopathic remedy for treating toothaches with shooting pains.
Dose: Weleda 6c.

EUPHRASIA
What it is: A homeopathic remedy for conjunctivitis with tears.
Dose: Nelsons 6c, Weleda 6c and 30c.

GRAPHITES
What it is: A homeopathic remedy for the treatment of a sty.
Dose: Weleda 6c and 30c, Nelsons 6c.

HEPAR SULPHURIS
What it is: A homeopathic remedy for relieving earaches.
Dose: Weleda 6c, Nelsons 6c, Ainsworth's 30c.

LALIUM MURIATICUM
What it is: A homeopathic remedy for relieving earaches caused by blocked Eustachian tubes.
Dose: New Era 6c.

MERCURIUS SOLUBILIS
What it is: A homeopathic remedy for the treatment of earaches, abscesses and bad breath.
Dose: Weleda 6c and 30c, Nelsons 6c, Ainsworth's 30c.

NATRUM MURIATICUM
What it is: A homeopathic remedy which can be used to treat viral skin conditions.
Dose: Weleda 6c, New Era 6x, Nelsons 6c, Ainsworth's 30c.

NELSONS CANDIDA
What it is: A treatment which can be used for Candida albicans (thrush) infections, including those affecting the mouth.
Dose: Adults should take two 6c tablets every hour for six doses, followed by two tablets three times a day. Children should be given half the adult dose.

PICKLE'S SOOTHAKE GEL
What it is: A gel for relieving toothache, containing clove oil and an antiseptic.
Dose: Apply to the tooth as required. Seek dental treatment if symptoms persist. This treatment is not suitable for children.

PICKLE'S SOOTHAKE TOOTHACHE TINCTURE

What it is: A tincture for relieving toothache, containing a mild anaesthetic.

Dose: Apply to the tooth to ease the pain as required.

RHUS TOXICODENDRON

What it is: A homeopathic remedy which can be used to treat viral skin conditions.

Dose: Weleda 6c and 30c, Nelsons 6c, Ainsworth's 30c.

SILICA

What it is: A homeopathic remedy for the treatment of abscesses.

Dose: Weleda 6c and 30c, Nelsons 6c, New Weleda 6c and 30c, Nelsons 6c, New Era 6x, Ainsworth's 30c.

THUJA

What it is: A homeopathic remedy for tooth decay which occurs at the roots.

Dose: Weleda 6c and 30c, Nelsons 6c.

REMEDIES FOR DISORDERS AFFECTING THE BLOOD AND CIRCULATORY SYSTEM

CALCAREA FLUORICA

What it is: A homeopathic remedy for the treatment of piles and varicose veins that promotes tissue elasticity.

Dose: Weleda 6c and 30c, Nelsons 6c, New Era 6x. This treatment is not suitable for children.

FERRUM PHOSPHORICUM

What it is: A homeopathic remedy for anaemia.

Dose: Weleda 6c and 30c, New Era 6x, Nelsons 6c. If anaemia persists, consult your doctor.

HAMAMELIS

What it is: A homeopathic remedy for the treatment of chilblains, piles and varicose veins.

Dose: Weleda 6c and 30c, Nelsons 6c. This treatment is not suitable for children.

LANES HEEMEX

What it is: An astringent ointment for relieving the discomfort of piles, containing witch hazel.

Dose: Apply the ointment morning and evening and after each bowel movement. Can cause allergy in some people. This treatment is not suitable for children.

NELSONS HAEMORRHOID CREAM
What it is: A herbal cream which can be used to soothe and treat the symptoms of piles, containing calendula, horse chestnut, witch hazel and paeonia officinalis.
Dose: Apply as needed. This treatment is not suitable for children.

NELSONS OINTMENT FOR CHILBLAINS
What it is: A homeopathic ointment for the treatment of unbroken chilblains, containing tamus communis 6x.
Dose: Weleda 6c and 30c, Nelsons 6c. This treatment is not suitable for children.

NEW ERA COMBINATION L
What it is: A homeopathic remedy for the treatment of varicose veins, containing calc fluor, ferr phos and nat mur.
Dose: The prepared remedy contains 6x of each of the above ingredients.

NUX VOMICA
What it is: A homeopathic remedy for itchy piles.
Dose: Weleda 6c and 30c, Nelsons 6c, Ainsworth's 30c. This treatment is not suitable for children.

PICKLE'S CHILBLAIN CREAM
What it is: A herbal cream for the treatment of chilblains, containing a rubefacient.
Dose: The cream should be applied sparingly morning and night and more frequently if required. This treatment is not suitable for pregnant or breastfeeding women.

PICKLE'S SNOWFIRE
What it is: A herbal ointment for the treatment of chilblains, containing benzoin, citronella and oils of thyme, clove and cade.
Dose: Apply to the affected area as required.

POTTER'S PILE TABS
What it is: A herbal tablet for relieving the symptoms of piles. The tablets have an astringent and laxative effect, and contain pilewort, cascara, agrimony and stone root.
Dose: Two tablets should be taken three times a day. The elderly should take two tablets twice a day. This treatment is not suitable for children or pregnant women.

POTTER'S PILEWORT OINTMENT
What it is: A herbal ointment for relieving the symptoms of piles, containing pilewort and lanolin.
Dose: The ointment should be applied twice a day. This treatment is not suitable for children and should not be used by anyone sensitive to lanolin.

POTTER'S VARICOSE OINTMENT
What it is: A herbal ointment for the treatment of varicose veins, containing cade oil, witch hazel and zinc oxide.
Dose: The ointment should be applied to the affected area twice a day. It should not be used on broken skin.

PULSATILLA
What it is: A homeopathic remedy for the treatment of varicose veins associated with poor circulation.
Dose: Weleda 6c and 30c, Nelsons 6c, Ainsworth's 30c.

WELEDA FROST CREAM
What it is: A homeopathic cream for relieving the symptoms of chilblains, containing balsam of Peru, rosemary oil and stibium metallicum.
Dose: The cream should be applied to the affected area several times a day. Can cause allergy, so a skin test should be carried out first.

REMEDIES FOR DISORDERS AFFECTING MENTAL HEALTH

ACTAEA RACEMOSA
What it is: A homeopathic remedy for the treatment of depression.
Dose: Weleda 6c, Nelsons 6c.

ARGENTUM NITRICUM
What it is: A homeopathic remedy for treating anxiety caused by nervousness or anticipatory fear.
Dose: Nelsons 6c, Weleda 6c and 30c.

ARSENICUM ALBUM
What it is: A homeopathic remedy for treating insomnia caused by an overactive mind and for anxiety with fear.
Dose: Weleda 6c and 30c, Nelsons 6c, Ainsworth's 30c.

AVENA SATIVA COMP
What it is: A liquid herbal remedy that has a sedative and analgesic effect. It can be used to treat irritability, tension, tension-induced aches and pains and sleep problems. Contains coffea, oats, passionflower and valerian.
Dose: Adults should take 10-20 drops in water 30 minutes before retiring. Children (2-12 years) should be given 5-10 drops. This treatment is not suitable for children under two years.

BIOPHYLLIN
What it is: A herbal tablet remedy which helps promote sleep and can be used to treat tension, restlessness and irritability. The tablets contain valerian, black cohosh, Jamaican dogwood and skullcap.
Dose: Two tablets should be taken after meals three times a day. This treatment is not suitable for children.

BIO-STRATH ELIXIR
What it is: A herbal elixir for alleviating fatigue and tiredness, containing yeast.
Dose: 5 ml should be taken three times a day before meals. This treatment is not suitable for children under 12 years.

BIO-STRATH VALERIAN FORMULA
What it is: A herbal liquid remedy which promotes natural sleep and can be used for relieving tension, irritability, stress and emotional strain. Contains passionflower, valerian, peppermint and yeast.
Dose: 20 drops should be diluted in water and taken three times a day before meals. This treatment is not suitable for children, and should not be combined with other homeopathic remedies.

CALCAREA CARBONICA
What it is: A homeopathic remedy for the treatment of insomnia.
Dose: Nelsons 6c, Weleda 6c and 30c.

CALCAREA PHOSPHORICA
What it is: A homeopathic remedy for alleviating fatigue in adolescents.
Dose: Weleda 6c, Nelsons 6c, New Era 6x.

CHAMOMILLA
What it is: A homeopathic remedy for treating insomnia which occurs as a result of pain or anger. This remedy is also available in drops.
Dose: Ainsworth's 30c, Weleda 3x and 30c.

COFFEA
What it is: A homeopathic remedy for treating insomnia caused by an

overactive mind.
Dose: Weleda 6c.

CURZON
What it is: A herbal stimulant in tablet form for relieving nervous strain. Contains damiana.
Dose: Two tablets should be taken at night and two in the morning. This treatment is not suitable for children under 12 years. This stimulant can cause side effects – always read the label.

FRAGADOR
What it is: A tablet remedy for relieving temporary irritability and emotional unrest, containing aniseed, conchae, lovage, sage, scurvy grass, stinging nettle, wheatgerm, wild strawberry, glycogen 10x, ferrum phosphoricum 4x, natrum carbonicum 1x and radix mel 1x.
Dose: Two tablets should be taken three times a day. This treatment is not suitable for children, and should not be combined with other homeopathic remedies.

GELSEMIUM
What it is: A homeopathic remedy for alleviating fatigue.
Dose: Weleda 6c, Nelsons 6c, Ainsworth's 30c.

HEATH & HEATHER BECALM
What it is: A tablet remedy with a sedative effect for relieving stress. The tablets contain hops, passionflower and valerian.
Dose: One tablet should be taken three times a day. This treatment is not suitable for children.

HEATH & HEATHER QUIET NIGHT TABLETS
What it is: A tablet remedy to aid sleep, containing hops, passionflower and valerian.
Dose: Two tablets one hour before bedtime. This treatment is not suitable for children.

HYPERICUM
What it is: A herbal remedy for treating mild depression made from the St John's wort plant.
Dose: Weleda 6c and 30c, Nelsons 6c, Ainsworth's 30c.

KALIUM PHOSPHORICUM
What it is: A homeopathic remedy for treating mild depression and nervous exhaustion.
Dose: Weleda 6c and 30c, Nelsons 6c, New Era 6x.

KALMS
What it is: A herbal tablet remedy which promotes natural sleep. Can be used to relieve the symptoms of anxiety, irritability and stress. Contains gentian, hops and valerian.
Dose: Two tablets should be taken three times a day after meals. This treatment is not suitable for children.

MOTHERWORT COMPOUND
What it is: A tablet remedy with a sedative effect for treating the symptoms of emotional stress and strain. Contains motherwort, limeflower and passionflower.
Dose: Two tablets should be taken three times a day after meals. This treatment is not suitable for children.

NATRACALM
What it is: A tablet remedy for relieving stress, strain and nervous tension, containing passionflower.
Dose: One tablet should be taken three times a day. This treatment is not suitable for children.

NATRASLEEP
What it is: A herbal tablet which promotes natural sleep, containing hops and valerian.
Dose: 1-3 tablets should be taken 30 minutes before bedtime. This treatment is not suitable for children.

NATRUM MURIATICUM
What it is: A homeopathic remedy for the treatment of mild depression.
Dose: Weleda 6c and 30c, New Era 6x, Nelsons 6c, Ainsworth's 30c.

NATUREST
What it is: A herbal tablet remedy for the treatment of temporary insomnia which occurs as a result of stress. Contains passiflora.
Dose: Two tablets should be taken three times a day and 1-3 tablets at bedtime. This treatment is not suitable for children.

NEW ERA COMBINATION B
What it is: A homeopathic remedy for alleviating general debility, containing calc phos, kali phos and ferr phos.
Dose: One tablet contains 6x of each of the above ingredients.

NOCTURA
What it is: A tablet remedy for treating insomnia, containing kali brom, coffea, passiflora, avena sativa, alfalfa and valeriana.
Dose: Two tablets should be taken four hours before bedtime

followed by two tablets immediately before bedtime. A further two tablets should be taken during the night, if required. One tablet contains 6c of each of the ingredients above. This treatment is not suitable for children.

NYTOL HERBAL
What it is: A tablet remedy for relieving temporary insomnia. Contains hops, passiflora, Jamaican dogwood, pulsatilla and wild lettuce.
Dose: Two tablets should be taken before bedtime. This treatment is not suitable for children.

POTTER'S ANA-SED
What it is: A sedative herbal remedy with an analgesic action that can be used to treat irritability, emotional stress and tension. Contains valerian, vervain, skullcap and hops.
Dose: Two tablets should be taken three times a day. This treatment is not suitable for children.

POTTER'S CHLOROPHYLL
What it is: A herbal stimulant in tablet form for relieving temporary tiredness. Contains chlorophyll and kola nut.
Dose: 1-2 tablets should be taken three times a day.

POTTER'S ELIXIR OF DAMIANA AND SAW PALMETTO
What it is: A restorative elixir containing saw palmetto, damiana and cornsilk.
Dose: 10 ml should be taken three times a day for seven days, reducing dose by half for the following seven days. This treatment is not suitable for children. This treatment can cause side effects – always read the label.

POTTER'S NODOFF PASSIFLORA TABLETS
What it is: A herbal tablet remedy which promotes sleep. The tablets contain passiflora.
Dose: Two tablets should be taken in early evening and two tablets before bedtime. This treatment is not suitable for children.

POTTER'S STRENGTH TABLETS
What it is: A herbal tablet stimulant for treating fatigue after illness. Contains damiana, kola and saw palmetto.
Dose: Two tablets should be taken three times a day. This treatment is not suitable for children. These tablets can cause side effects – always read the label.

QUIET LIFE
What it is: A tablet remedy with a mild sedative action for the

treatment of irritability, nervousness, tension and sleeplessness. The tablets contain hops, motherwort, passionflower, valerian, wild lettuce and vitamins B1, B2 and B3.

Dose: Two tablets should be taken twice a day, and 2-3 tablets before bedtime. This treatment is not suitable for children.

SEPIA
What it is: A homeopathic remedy for treating mild depression and tiredness.
Dose: Weleda 6c and 30c, Nelsons 6c, Ainsworth's 30c.

SERENITY
What it is: A tablet remedy for relieving emotional stress, strain and irritability. The tablets contain hops, passionflower and valerian.
Dose: Two tablets should be taken three times a day after food. This treatment is not suitable for children.

SOMNUS
What it is: A herbal tablet remedy which promotes natural sleep, containing hops, valerian and wild lettuce.
Dose: Two tablets should be taken one hour before bedtime. This treatment is not suitable for children.

SULPHUR
What it is: A homeopathic remedy which promotes deep natural sleep.
Dose: Ainsworth's 30c, Nelsons 6c, New Era 6c and 30c.

SUNERVEN
What it is: A tablet remedy for relieving anxiety, irritability, emotional stress, fatigue and insomnia. The tablets contain motherwort, passionflower, valerian and vervain.
Dose: Two tablets should be taken three times a day after meals and two tablets before bedtime. This treatment is not suitable for children.

VALERIAN COMPOUND
What it is: A herbal tablet remedy which promotes natural sleep, containing valerian, hops, Jamaican dogwood, passionflower and wild lettuce.
Dose: Two tablets should be taken in early evening followed by two just before retiring. This treatment is not suitable for children.

VALERINA DAY TABLETS
What it is: Tablets which relieve tension and irritability, containing valerian and lemon balm.
Dose: Two tablets should be taken three times a day. This treatment is not suitable for children. Also available as Valerian Night Tablets.

REMEDIES FOR DISORDERS AFFECTING THE FEMALE REPRODUCTIVE SYSTEM

ATHERA

What it is: A traditional herbal remedy for the relief of minor conditions associated with the menopause, such as water retention and constipation. It has a mild tonic effect and contains vervain, senna leaf, clivers and parsley root.

Dose: 2-3 tablets should be taken three times a day after meals. This treatment should not be used by pregnant or breastfeeding women.

CASCADE

What it is: A herbal tablet remedy for relieving pre-menstrual water retention. It has a diuretic action and contains clivers, burdock root and uva ursi.

Dose: Two tablets should be taken three times a day before meals.

HEATH & HEATHER WATER RELIEF

What it is: A herbal tablet remedy for relieving pre-menstrual water retention. It has a diuretic action and contains bladderwrack, burdock root, clivers and ground ivy.

Dose: 1-2 tablets up to three times a day for up to seven days, before a period is expected.

POTTER'S ANTITIS

What it is: A herbal tablet remedy for relieving the symptoms of cystitis.

Dose: Two tablets should be taken three times a day for a maximum of 10 days. The fluid intake should be increased while taking this remedy.

POTTER'S PREMENTAID

What it is: A diuretic and antispasmodic herbal tablet remedy with a mild, sedative effect for relieving pre-menstrual bloating and abdominal discomfort. It contains valerian, vervain, motherwort, uva ursi and wild anemone.

Dose: Two tablets should be taken three times a day when symptoms start prior to a period. Should not be used while taking sedative medications or alcohol.

POTTER'S RASPBERRY LEAF

What it is: A herbal tablet remedy for relieving painful menstrual cramps, with a toning and relaxing effect. Contains raspberry leaf.

Dose: Two tablets should be taken three times a day after meals.

POTTER'S WELLWOMAN

What it is: A herbal tablet remedy which promotes wellbeing in middle-aged women in pre-menopause and menopause. It contains valerian, lime flowers, motherwort, skullcap and yarrow.

Dose: Two tablets should be taken three times a day. This treatment should not be used while taking other sedative medications, and should not be used by pregnant women.

REMEDIES FOR DISORDERS AFFECTING THE SKIN

APIS MELLIFICA

What it is: A homeopathic remedy for relieving burning and stinging pains, and bites and stings that are red and swollen. It is made from honeybee venom.

Dose: Weleda 6c and 30c, Nelsons 6c, Ainsworth's 30c.

ARNICA

What it is: A homeopathic remedy for treating bruising.

Dose: Weleda 6c and 30c, Nelsons 6c, Ainsworth's 30c.

BELLADONNA

What it is: A homeopathic remedy for treating acne.

Dose: Weleda 6c and 30c, Nelsons 6c, Ainsworth's 30c.

BLUE FLAG ROOT COMPOUND

What it is: An antiseptic, anti-inflammatory herbal tablet remedy that is used to treat eczema and other skin conditions, containing blue flag root, burdock and sarsaparilla.

Dose: One tablet should be taken three times a day after meals. This treatment is not suitable for children under 12 years. Pregnant women should consult their doctor before using this product.

CALCAREA CARBONICA

What it is: A homeopathic remedy for the treatment of itchy and cracked skin.

Dose: Weleda 6c and 30c, Nelsons 6c.

CALCAREA FLUORICA

What it is: A homeopathic remedy which is used to promote tissue elasticity, scar and adhesion healing.

Dose: Weleda 6c and 30c, Nelsons 6c, New Era 6x.

CALCAREA PHOSPHORICA

What it is: A homeopathic remedy for the treatment of acne.

Dose: Weleda 6c and 30c, Nelsons 6c, Ainsworth's 30c.

CALCAREA SULPHURICA
What it is: A homeopathic remedy for treating acne, abscesses which have begun to emit discharge and any wounds that are healing slowly.
Dose: New Era 6x.

CANTHARIS
What it is: A homeopathic remedy for the treatment of minor burns.
Dose: Weleda 6c and 30c, Nelsons 6c, Ainsworth's 30c.

CAUSTICUM
What it is: A homeopathic remedy for the treatment of minor burns.
Dose: Weleda 6c.

DERMATODORON OINTMENT
What it is: A herbal ointment for relieving the symptoms of eczema, containing loosestrife and woody nightshade.
Dose: The ointment should be applied to the affected area two or three times a day.

GRAPHITES
What it is: A homeopathic remedy for the treatment of eczema where there is weeping and cracked skin.
Dose: Weleda 6c and 30c, Nelsons 6c.

HAMAMELIS
What it is: A homeopathic remedy for relieving sore, bruised skin.
Dose: Weleda 6c and 30c, Nelsons 6c.

HEATH & HEATHER SKIN TABLETS
What it is: A herbal tablet remedy for relieving the symptoms of skin blemishes and dry eczema, containing burdock root and wild pansy.
Dose: Two tablets should be taken three times a day. This treatment is not suitable for children. Pregnant women should consult their doctor before use.

HEPAR SULPHURIS
What it is: A homeopathic remedy which acts as a healing aid for eczema and for wounds that ooze.
Dose: Weleda 6c and 30c, Nelsons 6c, Ainsworth's 30c.

HERBHEAL OINTMENT
What it is: A soothing herbal ointment for relieving itchy skin complaints, containing chickweed, colophony, lanolin, marshmallow,

sulphur and zinc oxide.
Dose: The ointment should be applied to the affected area twice a day. This treatment is not suitable for children under five years.

HYPERICUM
What it is: A homeopathic remedy which promotes the healing of wounds which affect nerve endings.
Dose: Weleda 6c and 30c, Nelsons 6c.

KLEER TABLETS
What it is: A herbal tablet for the treatment of minor skin conditions and eczema. It contains burdock root, echinacea and stinging nettle.
Dose: Adults should take two tablets three times a day before meals. Children (5-12 years) should be given one tablet three times a day before meals. This treatment is not suitable for children under five years or for pregnant or breastfeeding women.

LEDUM
What it is: A homeopathic remedy for relieving the symptoms of insect bites, bee stings and puncture wounds.
Dose: Weleda 6c, Ainsworth's 30c.

MERCURIUS SOLUBILIS
What it is: A homeopathic remedy for the treatment of abscesses and boils.
Dose: Weleda 6c and 30c, Nelsons 6c, New Era 6x, Ainsworth's 30c.

NATRUM MURIATICUM
What it is: A homeopathic remedy for the treatment of eczema.
Dose: Weleda 6c and 30c, Nelsons 6c, New Era 6x, Ainsworth's 30c.

NELSONS ARNICA CREAM
What it is: A herbal cream remedy for relieving bruises, containing arnica.
Dose: The cream should be applied to the affected area as required.

NELSONS BURNS OINTMENT
What it is: A herbal ointment remedy for the treatment of minor burns. It contains calendula, echinacea, hypericum and urtica urens.
Dose: The ointment should be applied as required to the affected area which should then be covered with a dry dressing.

NELSONS CANDIDA
What it is: A homeopathic tablet remedy for the treatment of athlete's foot, containing Candida albicans 6c.
Dose: Adults should take two tablets every hour for six doses, then

reduce the dose to two tablets three times a day. Children should be given half the adult dose.

NELSONS GRAPHITES CREAM
What it is: A homeopathic remedy for the treatment of dermatitis, containing Graphites 6x.
Dose: The cream should be applied to the affected area as required.

NELSONS HYPERCAL
What it is: A herbal cream and tincture remedy for soothing and promoting the healing of sore skin and cuts. The cream contains calendula and hypericum.
Dose: The cream should be applied to the affected area. Can be diluted 1 part cream to 10 parts water and then applied to larger wounds.

NELSONS PYRETHRUM
What it is: A herbal liquid remedy for soothing hives, insect bites and stings, containing pyrethrum, arnica, calendula, echinacea, hypericum, ledum palustre and rumex crispus.
Dose: The liquid should be applied to the affected area as soon as possible after a bite or sting has occurred. This treatment is also available in spray form.

NEW ERA ELASTO
What it is: A homeopathic remedy to promote the formation of elastic, responsible for the repair and health of tissues in the body. Contains 6x of each of the following – calc fluor, calc phos, ferr phos and mag phos.
Dose: One tablet provides 6x of each of the above ingredients.

PHOSPHORUS
What it is: A homeopathic remedy which can be used to prevent bruising, particularly in those who are prone to it.
Dose: Weleda 6c and 30c, Nelsons 6c, Ainsworth's 30c.

POTTER'S ADIANTINE
What it is: A herbal remedy for the treatment of dandruff and for improving hair condition. It contains bay oil, rosemary, southernwood and witch hazel.
Dose: The liquid should be massaged into the scalp morning and evening. This treatment is not suitable for children.

POTTER'S COMFREY OINTMENT
What it is: A herbal ointment remedy for the relief and treatment of sprains and bruises. It contains comfrey.
Dose: The ointment should be applied to the affected area twice a day

after bathing. This treatment should not be used for more than 10 days.

POTTER'S ECZEMA OINTMENT
What it is: A herbal ointment for relieving the symptoms of eczema, containing benzoic acid, salicylic acid, zinc oxide, lanolin and chickweed.
Dose: The ointment should be applied to the affected area twice a day. This treatment is not suitable for children under five years.

POTTER'S ERUPTIONS MIXTURE
What it is: A herbal mixture for treating the symptoms of mild eczema, containing blue flag, buchu, burdock root, cascara, sarsaparilla and yellow dock.
Dose: Adults should take 5 ml three times a day. Children over eight years should be given 5 ml every 12 hours. This treatment is not suitable for children under eight years. Pregnant or breastfeeding women should consult their doctor before using this product.

POTTER'S EXTRACT OF ROSEMARY
What it is: A herbal liquid for improving general hair condition which can also be used to treat mild dandruff. Contains bay oil, rosemary, rose geranium and methyl salicylate.
Dose: The liquid should be massaged into the scalp twice a day until symptoms clear. This treatment is not suitable for children.

POTTER'S SKIN CLEAR OINTMENT
What it is: An astringent and mild antiseptic ointment for relieving the symptoms of mild acne and eczema. It contains sulphur, tea tree oil and zinc oxide.
Dose: The ointment should be applied twice a day to the affected areas. This treatment is not suitable for children under five years.

POTTER'S SKIN CLEAR TABLETS
What it is: A herbal tablet remedy for the relief and prevention of minor skin blemishes and acne. It contains echinacea.
Dose: Two tablets should be taken three times a day. This treatment is not suitable for children, or for pregnant or breastfeeding women.

RHUS TOXICODENDRON
What it is: A homeopathic remedy for the treatment of eczema.
Dose: Weleda 6c and 30c, Nelsons 6c, Ainsworth's 30c.

SILICA
What it is: A homeopathic remedy for the treatment of abscesses, boils and athlete's foot.
Dose: Weleda 6c and 30c, Nelsons 6c, New Era 6x, Ainsworth's 30c.

SULPHUR
What it is: A homeopathic remedy for the treatment of eczema, acne and slow healing burns.
Dose: Weleda 6c and 30c, Nelsons 6c, Ainsworth's 30c.

THUJA
What it is: A homeopathic remedy for the treatment of warts.
Dose: Weleda 6c and 30c, Nelsons 6c.

URTICA URENS
What it is: A homeopathic remedy for the treatment of minor burns where blistering has not occurred.
Dose: Weleda 6c.

WELEDA ARNICA OINTMENT
What it is: A herbal ointment which can be used to relieve muscular pains, stiffness, strains and bruises. It contains arnica.
Dose: The ointment should be massaged into the affected area three to four times a day. This treatment is also available in lotion form.

WELEDA BALSAMICUM OINTMENT
What it is: A herbal ointment which promotes the healing of boils and minor wounds. It contains balsam of Peru, marigold, dog's mercury, metallicum preparatum and stibium.
Dose: The ointment should be applied directly to the affected area or placed on a dressing which will be applied to the boil or wound. Repeat as necessary. The treatment should be discontinued immediately if there is any adverse reaction of the skin.

WELEDA CALENDOLON OINTMENT
What it is: An antiseptic herbal remedy for the treatment of cuts and minor wounds, containing marigold.
Dose: The ointment should be applied to the affected area 2-3 times a day. It should not be applied to infected wounds. Pregnant women should consult their doctor prior to use.

WELEDA CALENDULA LOTION
What it is: A herbal lotion for the treatment of minor skin wounds, containing marigold.
Dose: 5 ml of the liquid should be added to boiled water and allowed to cool. The lotion can be used to clean wounds or applied to dressings over the affected area. It should not be used on wounds which are infected. Pregnant women should consult a pharmacist or doctor before using this product.

WELEDA COMBUDORON LOTION

What it is: A herbal lotion for the treatment and relief of minor burns, containing arnica and small nettle.

Dose: 5 ml of the lotion should be added to a cup of cooled boiled water, then used to moisten a pad which should be applied to the burn as a compress and kept moist. This treatment is also available in ointment form.

WELEDA WCS DUSTING POWDER

What it is: A herbal powder remedy for the treatment of minor burns. It contains arnica, echinacea, marigold, silica, stibium and metallicum praep.

Dose: The powder should be applied to the affected area and covered with a dry dressing. The dressing should be changed twice a day.

REMEDIES FOR DISORDERS AFFECTING BONES AND MUSCLES

ACTAEA RACEMOSA

What it is: A homeopathic remedy for relieving stiff neck, rheumatic pains in the back and neck and muscle ache brought on by exercise.

Dose: Weleda 6c and 30c, Nelsons 6c.

APIS MELLIFICA

What it is: A homeopathic remedy for the treatment of arthritis with red and swollen joints and hot, red swellings in the body.

Dose: Weleda 6c and 30c, Nelsons 6c, Ainsworth's 30c.

ARNICA

What it is: A homeopathic remedy for relieving sprains and aching muscles.

Dose: Weleda 6x, 6c and 30c, Nelsons 6c, Ainsworth's 30c.

BELLADONNA PLASTER

What it is: An adhesive plaster impregnated with a rubefacient for relieving muscular and rheumatic pains, strains, stiffness and lumbago. Contains belladonna alkaloids.

Dose: The plaster should be applied to the affected area and left on for two to three days. This treatment is not suitable for children under 10 years.

BIO-STRATH WILLOW FORMULA

What it is: A herbal liquid remedy for relieving muscular pain, backache, lumbago, sciatica and fibrosis. It contains willow bark, primula and yeast.

Dose: 1.5 ml should be diluted in water three times a day before meals. This treatment is not suitable for children.

BRYONIA
What it is: A homeopathic remedy for relieving arthritis and sharp pains.
Dose: Weleda 6c and 30c, Nelsons 6c, Ainsworth's 30c.

CALCAREA FLUORICA
What it is: A homeopathic remedy for relieving arthritis that responds to warmth and movement.
Dose: Weleda 6c and 30c, Nelsons 6c, New Era 6x.

COLOCYNTHIS
What it is: A homeopathic remedy for alleviating cramps and spasms, particularly those occurring in the calves.
Dose: Weleda 6c.

DRAGON BALM OINTMENT
What it is: A herbal ointment for relieving rheumatism and other joint problems. It contains balsam of Peru, camphor, cassia, eucalyptus, guaiacum, nutmeg, turpentine and thymol.
Dose: The ointment should be applied to the affected area as required. This treatment is not suitable for children under six years.

FERRUM PHOSPHORICUM
What it is: A homeopathic remedy for relieving rheumatism.
Dose: Weleda 6c and 30c, Nelsons 6c, New Era 6x, Ainsworth's 30c.

GERARD HOUSE CELERY TABLETS
What it is: A herbal tablet for relieving the symptoms of rheumatic pain, containing celery.
Dose: Should be used according to the instructions on the label, according to symptoms. This treatment is not suitable for children.

GERARD HOUSE LIGVITES
What it is: A herbal tablet for relieving the symptoms of rheumatic pain, stiffness, backache and lumbago. Each tablet contains black cohosh, guaiacum, poplar bark, sarsaparilla and white willow bark.
Dose: Two tablets should be taken twice a day with food. This treatment is not suitable for children under 12 years.

GONNE BALM
What it is: A herbal remedy for relieving muscular aches and pains such as general stiffness, backache, sciatica and lumbago. The balm contains camphor, eucalyptus oil, levo-menthol, methyl salicylate (an aspirin derivative) and turpentine.
Dose: The balm should be massaged into the affected area two to three

times a day, and once during the night if necessary. This treatment is not suitable for children under 12 years.

HEATH & HEATHER RHEUMATIC PAIN TABLETS
What it is: A herbal tablet remedy for relieving the symptoms of backache, lumbago, fibrositis and rheumatic pain. Each tablet contains bogbean, guaiacum and celery.
Dose: One tablet should be taken three times a day. This treatment is not suitable for children.

KALIUM MURIATICUM
What it is: A homeopathic remedy for the treatment of rheumatic swelling.
Dose: New Era 6x.

KALIUM SULPHURICUM
What it is: A homeopathic remedy for the treatment of rheumatism that moves from joint to joint.
Dose: New Era 6x.

LEDUM
What it is: A homeopathic remedy for the treatment of rheumatism that moves from joint to joint.
Dose: New Era 6x.

MAGNESIA PHOSPHORICA
What it is: A homeopathic remedy for relieving sciatica, cramp and muscular spasms.
Dose: New Era 6x.

NATRUM PHOSPHORICUM
What it is: A homeopathic remedy which assists the removal of excess lactic acid in the body in order to ease rheumatic conditions.
Dose: New Era 6x.

NELSONS OINTMENT FOR STRAINS
What it is: A herbal ointment for relieving strains and sprains, containing ruta graveolens.
Dose: The ointment should be applied to the affected area as required.

NELSONS RHEUMATICA
What it is: A homeopathic remedy for relieving rheumatic pains, containing rhus toxicodendron 6c.
Dose: Adults should take two tablets every hour for six doses, followed by two tablets three times a day. Children should be given half the adult dose.

NELSONS RHUS TOX CREAM

What it is: A herbal cream for relieving rheumatic pains and strains, containing rhus toxicodendron.
Dose: The cream should be massaged into the affected area as required.

NEW ERA COMBINATION A

What it is: A homeopathic remedy for relieving sciatica, containing ferr phos, kali phos and mag phos.
Dose: Contains 6x of each of the above ingredients.

NEW ERA COMBINATION G

What it is: A homeopathic remedy for the treatment of backache and lumbar pain, containing calc fluor, calc phos, kali phos and nat mur.
Dose: Contains 6x of each of the above ingredients.

NEW ERA COMBINATION 1

What it is: A homeopathic remedy for the treatment of muscular pain and fibrositis, containing ferr phos, kali sulph and mag phos.
Dose: Contains 6x of each of the above ingredients.

NEW ERA COMBINATION P

What it is: A homeopathic remedy for relieving aching legs and feet, containing calc fluor, calc phos, kali phos and mag phos.
Dose: Contains 6x of each of the above ingredients.

OLBAS OIL

What it is: An oil for the treatment of muscular pain and stiffness. It contains oils of cajuput, clove, eucalyptus, juniper berry, menthol, mint and wintergreen and acts as an analgesic and rubefacient.
Dose: The oil should be massaged into the affected area three times a day. This treatment is not suitable for children.

PHYTOLACCA

What it is: A homeopathic remedy for relieving rheumatism and shooting pains in the body.
Dose: Weleda 6c.

POTTER'S BACKACHE TABLETS

What it is: A herbal tablet remedy for relieving back pain. Each tablet contains buchu, gravel root, hydrangea and uva ursi.
Dose: Two tablets should be taken three times a day. This treatment is not suitable for children.

POTTER'S COMFREY OINTMENT

What it is: A herbal ointment for relieving sprains and bruises, containing comfrey.
Dose: The cream should be applied to the affected area twice a day after

bathing and should not be used for more than 10 days.

POTTER'S NINE RUBBING OILS
What it is: A 9 oil herbal mix rubefacient used for easing the symptoms of muscular pain and stiffness including backache, sciatica, lumbago, fibrositis and rheumatic pains. It contains amber, arachis, clove, eucalyptus, mustard, menthyl salicylate (an aspirin derivative), linseed, peppermint and turpentine.
Dose: The oil should be rubbed into the affected area as required. This treatment should not be combined with other homeopathic remedies.

POTTER'S RHEUMATIC PAIN TABLETS
What it is: A herbal tablet for relieving rheumatic aches and pains. Each tablet contains bogbean, burdock, guaiacum, nutmeg and yarrow.
Dose: Two tablets should be taken three times a day. This treatment is not suitable for children and should not be used if suffering from diarrhoea.

POTTER'S SCIARGO
What it is: A herbal tablet with anti-inflammatory properties for relieving sciatica and lumbago. The tablets contain clivers, juniper berry, shepherd's purse, uva ursi and wild carrot.
Dose: Two tablets should be taken three times a day. This treatment is not suitable for children. Also available in the form of teabags.

POTTER'S TABRITIS
What it is: A herbal tablet with analgesic and anti-inflammatory properties for relieving the symptoms of rheumatism and stiffness. Each tablet contains clivers, burdock, elderflower, prickly ash bark, uva ursi and yarrow.
Dose: Two tablets should be taken three times a day. This treatment is not suitable for children.

PULSATILLA
What it is: A homeopathic remedy for relieving arthritis.
Dose: Weleda 6c and 30c, Nelsons 6c, Ainsworth's 30c.

REUMALEX
What it is: A herbal tablet for relieving rheumatic aches and pains. Contains black cohosh, guaiacum, poplar bark, sarsaparilla and white willow bark.
Dose: Two tablets should be taken twice a day. This treatment is not suitable for children.

RHEUMASOL
What it is: A herbal tablet remedy for relieving joint or muscle pain and stiffness. It contains guaiacum resin and prickly ash bark.

Dose: One tablet should be taken three times a day with meals. This treatment is not suitable for children.

RHUS TOXICODENDRON
What it is: A homeopathic remedy for the treatment of muscular strains, sprains, joint stiffness, rheumatism, arthritis and sciatica.
Dose: Weleda 6c and 30c, Nelsons 6c, Ainsworth's 30c.

RUTA GRAVEOLENS
What it is: A homeopathic remedy for the treatment of muscular strains, sprains, rheumatism, tennis elbow, tendon injuries and aching limbs when rhus toxicodendron is found to be ineffective.
Dose: Weleda 6c and 30c, Nelsons 6c, Ainsworth's 30c.

SYMPHYTUM
What it is: A homeopathic remedy for relieving cartilage injuries and old, painful injuries.
Dose: Weleda 6c.

VEGETEX
What it is: A herbal tablet for relieving rheumatic pain, fibrositis and lumbago. Each tablet contains black cohosh, buckbean and celery.
Dose: Three tablets should be taken three times a day with meals. This treatment is not suitable for children.

WELEDA ARNICA OINTMENT
What it is: A herbal ointment for relieving muscular pains, stiffness, strains and bruises. It contains arnica.
Dose: The ointment should be massaged gently into the affected area three or four times a day. This treatment is also available in the form of a lotion.

WELEDA COPPER OINTMENT
What it is: A herbal ointment remedy for relieving muscular rheumatic pain, containing cuprum metallicum praep.
Dose: The ointment should be applied to the affected area once or twice a day.

WELEDA MASSAGE BALM WITH ARNICA
What it is: A herbal balm for relieving the symptoms of rheumatic pain, muscular aches and pains, stiffness, backache, fibrositis and muscle cramps. It contains arnica, lavender, rosemary and silver birch.
Dose: The balm should be massaged into the affected area 3-4 times a day.

WELEDA RHEUMADORON DROPS
What it is: A herbal liquid for easing muscular rheumatic pain,

containing arnica, aconite, birch and mandragora root.

Dose: 5-10 drops should be taken 3-4 times a day.

WELEDA RHEUMADORON OINTMENT

What it is: A herbal ointment for easing muscular rheumatic pain, containing arnica, birch, mandrake, rosemary and wolfbane.

Dose: The ointment should be massaged into the affected area twice a day.

WELEDA RHUS TOX OINTMENT

What it is: A herbal ointment for relieving rheumatic pain, containing rhus toxicodendron.

Dose: The ointment may be applied directly to the affected area, or applied to a dressing and wrapped over the area.

WELEDA RUTA OINTMENT

What it is: A herbal ointment for relieving the pain and promoting the healing of strains and sprains. Contains rue tincture.

Dose: The ointment may be applied directly to the affected area or smeared on a dressing and wrapped over the area.

REMEDIES FOR DISORDERS AFFECTING CHILDREN

BIOBALM POWDER

What it is: A herbal powder for relieving wind and stomach upset, containing camomile, Irish bark, marshmallow root and slippery elm.

Dose: Half to one teaspoon mixed with water should be taken up to four times a day. This treatment is not suitable for children under five years.

CHAMOMILLA

What it is: A liquid homeopathic remedy for relieving the symptoms of colic and teething.

Dose: Ainsworth's 30c, Weleda 3x and 30c.

WELEDA BALSAMICUM OINTMENT

What it is: A herbal ointment remedy for treating nappy rash. Contains balsam of Peru, dog's mercury, marigold (calendula) and stibium metallicum preparatum.

Dose: The ointment should be applied to clean, dry skin several times a day.

WELEDA CAMOMILLA

What it is: A homeopathic remedy that is suitable for children or babies who are teething or suffering from colic or irritability.

Dose: 3x and 30c

OVER-THE COUNTER MEDICINES

Over-the-Counter (OTC) medicines are those which can be bought from either a pharmacist or other retail outlet, without the need for a prescription from a doctor.

Medicines which are available OTC are relatively mild and designed to help with the treatment of minor ailments at home. Many of the available products are not 'cures' but aim to relieve the symptoms of the problem so that the illness can run its course. For example, the many cold remedies available OTC do not attack the virus that causes colds, but relieve the sufferer of the discomfort of symptoms, such as sore throat or headache.

The minor conditions which are generally suitable for treatment with OTC medicines include: aches and pains, constipation and diarrhoea, coughs and colds, travel sickness, tummy upsets, skin conditions and low-grade infections such as thrush and cystitis.

However, as with all types of medicines, OTC products can be harmful or simply ineffective if they are not used, stored and disposed of properly. For this reason they should be treated with the same care as prescription medicines or any other dangerous chemicals you may keep in the house.

When buying OTC preparations it is worth making use of the expertise of a pharmacist. Pharmacists are trained, independent professionals who are willing to answer questions or give advice about the suitability of the medicines they sell. When you are discussing the suitability of a particular treatment with a pharmacist, ensure that you tell them about any prescription drugs you are taking or any other illnesses or allergies you, or the patient, may have.

When you are preparing to take the medicine, or to give it to someone else, always ensure that you read the packet carefully, taking note of how much you should take, when, and any other specific instructions such as whether it should be taken with food. Do not take any medication when you are pregnant or breastfeeding without first taking advice. Take extra care when giving medicines to children – they are not mini adults and their doses need to be carefully calculated by experts. Follow the advice on the packet or, if in doubt, ask your pharmacist.

Finally, but most importantly, remember to dispose of any unused medicines carefully and safely.

HOW TO USE THIS SECTION

The aim of this section is to give some basic information about the range of Over-the-Counter preparations available. The information is intended as guidance only and does not provide all you need to know about a product before deciding whether or not to use it. Most importantly, it should not be used as a substitute for talking to a qualified professional, and any queries you may have about a particular medicine should be addressed either to your GP or a pharmacist. Be aware, too, that OTC medicines should not be used by certain groups of people – for example, children of a certain age or people with long-standing conditions such as asthma or diabetes.

The most commonly used OTC products are listed below in alphabetical order, with the information arranged as follows:

Name: The branded name under which the product is sold.
Use: A brief description of the disorder the product treats and how it works.
Dose: The frequency and amount of each dose or, in the case of creams and lotions, each application.

AAA SPRAY

Use: An aerosol spray for soothing sore throats. It contains benzocaine, a local anaesthetic.
Dose: Adults should apply two sprays every 2-3 hours. The maximum dose is 16 sprays over 24 hours. For children over six years, half the adult dose should be given, with a maximum of 8 sprays over 24 hours. This treatment is not recommended for children under six years.

ACNE-AID

Use: A cleansing bar for the treatment of acne and greasy skin.
Dose: The cleansing bar should be used in the same way as an ordinary soap. This treatment is not recommended for children under 15 years.

ACIDEX

Use: A suspension containing sodium bicarbonate, sodium alginate and calcium carbonate. Alleviates heartburn, including heartburn of pregnancy, dyspepsia associated with gastric reflux, hiatus hernia, reflux oesophagitis, regurgitation and all cases of epigastric and retrosternal distress where the underlying cause is gastric reflux.
Dose: Adults and children over 12 years should take 10 ml-20 ml. Children 6-12 years 5 ml-10 ml. Doses should be taken after meals and at bedtime. This treatment is not recommended for children under 6

years. Contains 141 mg sodium in 10 ml, therefore use with caution in patients on sodium restricted diet. Do not take within two hours of taking other medicines.

ACNIDAZIL

Use: A cream for the treatment of acne, containing benzoyl peroxide and micanazole, an anti-microbial.

Dose: The cream should be applied to clean, dry skin once a day for the first week. In the second week it should be applied twice a day, and then for 4-8 weeks. This treatment is not recommended for children under 15 years.

ACRIFLEX CREAM

Use: A cream for the treatment of minor burns, cuts and grazes, containing chlorhexidine, an antiseptic.

Dose: The cream should be smoothed onto the affected area and then applied again after 15 minutes if required.

ACTAL

Use: Available in tablet form for relieving indigestion and settle digestive discomfort. The tablets contain an antacid.

Dose: 1-2 tablets should be taken as required. The maximum dose is 16 tablets over 24 hours. This treatment is not recommended for children under 12 years.

ACTIFED

Use: These are tablets for hayfever that contain triprolidine, an antihistamine, and pseudoephedrine, a decongestant.

Dose: One tablet should be taken up to four times a day. This treatment is not recommended for children under 12 years.

ACTIFED COMPOUND LINCTUS

Use: This is a liquid remedy for the treatment of coughs, containing dextromethorphan, a cough suppressant, pseudoephedrine, a decongestant and triprolidine, an antihistamine.

Dose: Adults should take 10 ml every four to six hours. Children (6-12 years) should be given 5 ml every 4-6 hours. Children (2-5 years) should be given 2.5 ml every four to six hours. Take a maximum of four doses in 24 hours. This treatment is not recommended for children under two years.

ACTIFED EXPECTORANT

Use: A liquid remedy for the treatment of coughs. It contains guaiphenesin, an expectorant, pseudoephedrine, a decongestant and an antihistamine.

Dose: Adults should take 10 ml every four to six hours. Children (6-

12 years) should be given 5 ml every 4-6 hours. Children (2-5 years) should be given 2.5 ml every 4-6 hours. This treatment is not recommended for children under two years.

ACTIFED SYRUP
Use: A liquid remedy for relieving cold, flu and hayfever symptoms. It contains triprolidine, an antihistamine and pseudoephedrine, a decongestant.
Dose: Adults should take 10 ml every 4-6 hours, with a maximum of 4 doses over 24 hours. Children (2-12 years) should be given 2.5-10 ml, according to age. Always read the label. This treatment is not recommended for children under two years. This product is also available in tablet form.

ADCORTYL IN ORABASE
Use: Available in the form of a paste for the treatment of mouth ulcers, containing triamcinolone, a corticosteroid.
Dose: The paste should be applied to the affected area up to three times a day after meals, and then once at night. The treatment can be used for up to five days.

ADULT MELTUS DRY COUGH ELIXIR
Use: A liquid remedy for the treatment of coughs, containing dextromethorphan, a suppressant, and pseudoephedrine, a decongestant.
Dose: Adults should take 5-10 ml four times a day. This treatment is not recommended for children under 12 years.

ADULT MELTUS EXPECTORANT
Use: A liquid remedy for the treatment of coughs, containing guaiphenesin, an expectorant, cetylp yearidium, an antiseptic, purified honey and sucrose.
Dose: Adults should take 5-10 ml every 3-4 hours. This treatment is not recommended for children under 12 years.

ADULT MELTUS EXPECTORANT WITH DECONGESTANT
Use: A liquid remedy for the treatment of coughs, containing guaiphenesin, an expectorant, and pseudoephedrine, a decongestant.
Dose: 10 ml should be taken four times a day. This treatment is not recommended for children under 12 years.

ADVIL COLD AND SINUS TABLETS
Use: These are tablets for relieving cold and flu symptoms, containing ibuprofen and pseudoephedrine, a decongestant.
Dose: 1-2 tablets should be taken every 4-6 hours. Take a maximum

of six tablets over 24 hours. This treatment is not recommended for children under 12 years.

ADVIL EXTRA STRENGTH IBUPROFEN
Use: Analgesic tablets which can be used for general pain relief, containing 400 mg ibuprofen.
Dose: One tablet, which can be taken up to three times a day. A maximum of three tablets can be taken over 24 hours. This treatment is not recommended for children under 12 years.

ADVIL IBUPROFEN
Use: These are analgesic tablets for general pain relief containing 200 mg ibuprofen.
Dose: 1-2 tablets should be taken with or just after a meal every 4-6 hours. Take a maximum of six tablets over 24 hours. This treatment is not recommended for children under 12 years.

AFRAZINE NASAL SPRAY
Use: This is a spray for clearing nasal congestion caused by a cold, sinusitis or hayfever. It contains oxymetazoline, a decongestant.
Dose: Adults and children over 5 years should apply 2-3 sprays into each nostril morning and night. The spray should not be used continuously for more than one week. This treatment is not recommended for children under 5 years.

AFTER BITE
Use: A pen that dispenses ammonia for soothing bites, stings and irritated or itchy skin.
Dose: The pen should be applied as often as required. This treatment is not recommended for children under 2 years.

ALGESAL
Use: A cream rub which can be applied to the skin to alleviate muscular aches and pains. It contains a rubefacient and salicylate, an aspirin derivative.
Dose: The cream should be massaged into the affected part of the body up to three times a day. This treatment is not recommended for children under six years.

ALGICON
Use: Available in tablet form for easing the symptoms of acidic stomach, heartburn and indigestion. The tablets contain antacids and an alginate. They have a high sugar content, so diabetics should check with a doctor prior to use.
Dose: 1-2 tablets should be taken four times a day after meals and on retiring. This treatment is not recommended for children under 12

years. The product is also available in liquid form.

ALGIPAN RUB
Use: A cream rub for the treatment of muscular aches and pains, containing rubefacients and a salicylate, an aspirin derivative.
Dose: The cream should be rubbed into the affected area 2-3 times a day. This treatment is not recommended for children under six years.

ALKA-SELTZER
Use: Effervescent tablets which contain an antacid and an analgesic for the relief of headache and upset stomach caused by excess alcohol or over-eating. The tablets contain 324 mg of aspirin, sodium bicarbonate and citric acid.
Dose: Two tablets should be dissolved in water every four hours. The maximum dose is eight tablets over 24 hours. This treatment is not recommended for children under 12 years.

ALKA-SELTZER XS
Use: Effervescent tablets containing an antacid and an analgesic for the relief of headache, upset stomach and general pain caused by excess alcohol or over-eating. The tablets contain 267 mg of aspirin, 133 mg of paracetamol, sodium bicarbonate, citric acid and caffeine.
Dose: 1-2 tablets should be dissolved in water. The maximum dosage is eight tablets over 24 hours. This treatment is not recommended for children under 12 years.

ALLER-EZE CREAM
Use: A cream for relieving itching and irritation caused by bites, stings and rashes. It contains clemastine, an antihistamine.
Dose: This treatment should be applied as and when required.

ALLER-EZE ORIGINAL FORMULA
Use: Available in tablet form for relieving the symptoms of hayfever. The tablets contain clemastine, an antihistamine.
Dose: Adults should take one tablet in the morning and one at night. For children (3-12 years), read the label for variations in dosage. This treatment is not recommended for children under three years.

ALLER-EZE PLUS
Use: These are tablets for relieving the symptoms of hayfever. They contain clemastine, an antihistamine and phenylpropanolamine, a decongestant.
Dose: One tablet should be taken every six hours. There is a maximum dose of four tablets over 24 hours. This treatment is not recommended for children under 12 years.

ALPHOSYL SHAMPOO 2-IN-1

Use: This is a medicated shampoo for the treatment of dandruff. It contains coal tar and a hair conditioner.
Dose: Apply as an ordinary shampoo every 2-3 days.

ALPKA KERI BATH OIL
Use: This is an emollient bath additive containing various oils, including lanolin, for the relief and treatment of eczema and dermatitis.
Dose: Should be added to bath water.

ALTACITE
Use: Available in tablet form for the relief of indigestion and heartburn.
Dose: Adults should take two tablets between meals and on retiring. Children (6-12 years) should take half the adult dose. This treatment is not recommended for children under six years.

ALTACITE PLUS
Use: These are antacid tablets for the relief of indigestion and heartburn. They contain dimethicone to aid the release of trapped wind.
Dose: Adults should take two tablets between meals and on retiring. Children (8-12 years) should take one tablet between meals and one at bedtime. This treatment is not recommended for children under eight years.

ALUDROX
Use: These are antacid tablets for the relief of indigestion and heartburn.
Dose: Adults should take 1-2 tablets four times a day and on retiring. Children (6-12 years) should take one tablet 2-3 times a day. This treatment is not recommended for children under six years. The product is also available in liquid form.

ANACAL RECTAL OINTMENT
Use: An ointment for the treatment and relief of piles. It contains mucopolysaccharide, which is thought to strengthen tissue in the anus.
Dose: The ointment should be applied to the affected area 1-4 times a day. This treatment is not recommended for children under 12 years.

ANACAL SUPPOSITORIES
Use: A treatment for piles available in the form of a suppository tablet. It contains mucopolysaccharide, which is thought to strengthen the tissue in the anus.
Dose: Insert one suppository once or twice a day. This treatment is not recommended for children under 12 years.

ANADIN
Use: Analgesic tablets which can be used for general pain relief, containing 325mg of aspirin, and caffeine.
Dose: Adults should take 1-2 tablets every four hours. The maximum dose is 12 tablets over 24 hours. This treatment is not recommended for children under 12 years.

ANADIN MAXIMUM STRENGTH
Use: Analgesic capsules which can be used for general pain relief, containing 500mg of aspirin, and caffeine.
Dose: Adults should take 1-2 capsules every four hours. There is a maximum dose of eight capsules over 24 hours. This treatment is not recommended for children under 12 years.

ANADIN EXTRA
Use: Analgesic tablets which can be used for general pain relief, containing 300mg of aspirin and 200 mg of paracetamol.
Dose: Adults should take two tablets every four hours. There is a maximum dose of eight tablets over 24 hours. This treatment is not recommended for children under 12 years. The product is also available in the form of soluble tablets with caffeine.

ANADIN IBUPROFEN
Use: Analgesic tablets which can be used for general pain relief, containing 200mg of ibuprofen.
Dose: Adults should take 1-2 tablets 2-3 times a day. There is a maximum dose of six tablets over 24 hours. This treatment is not recommended for children under 12 years.

ANADIN PARACETAMOL
Use: Analgesic tablets which can be used for general pain relief and contains 500mg of paracetamol.
Dose: Adults should take two tablets every four hours. There is a maximum dose of eight tablets over 24 hours. Children (6-12 years) should take half to one tablet every four hours. This treatment is not recommended for children under six years.

ANBESOL
Use: This treatment is available in liquid form for the relief and treatment of mouth ulcers. It contains lidocaine, an anaesthetic, and chlorocresol and cetylp yearidium, which are antiseptics.
Dose: Two applications to the affected area, allowing at least 30 minutes between applications. Use a maximum of eight applications over 24 hours.

ANBESOL ADULT STRENGTH GEL

Use: A gel for the relief and treatment of mouth ulcers. It contains lidocaine, an anaesthetic, and chlorocresol and cetylp yearidium, which are antiseptics.

Dose: Adults should apply the gel up to four times a day for one week. This treatment is not recommended for young children.

ANBESOL TEETHING GEL

Use: A gel for the relief of teething pain in babies, containing lidocaine, an anaesthetic, and various antiseptics.

Dose: The gel should be applied onto the affected area no more than four times a day.

ANDREWS ANTACID

Use: Available in tablet form for relieving the symptoms of upset stomach, indigestion and heartburn. The tablets contain various antacids.

Dose: Adults should take 1-2 tablets as needed. The maximum dose is 12 tablets over 24 hours. This treatment is not recommended for children under 12 years. The product is available in various flavours.

ANDREWS ORIGINAL SALTS

Use: Available in powder form for relieving an upset stomach. It contains antacids and sodium.

Dose: Adults should take one teaspoon or one sachet dissolved in water. Take a maximum of four doses over 24 hours. Children over three years should be given half the adult dose. This treatment is not recommended for children under three years.

ANETHAINE

Use: Available in the form of a cream for the treatment and relief of itching and irritation caused by bites and stings, containing a mild anaesthetic.

Dose: The cream should be applied to the affected area 2-3 times a day for up to three days. This treatment is not recommended for children under three years.

ANODESYN OINTMENT

Use: This is an ointment for the treatment of piles, containing benzocaine, a mild local anaesthetic, and allantoin, an astringent.

Dose: Adults should use the ointment twice a day and after each bowel movement. This treatment is not recommended for children under 12 years. The cream should not be used for more than one week unless advised otherwise by a doctor.

ANODESYN SUPPOSITORIES

Use: A suppository for the treatment and relief of piles, containing lignocaine, a mild local anaesthetic, and allantoin, an astringent.

Dose: Insert one suppository in the morning and one in the evening, and after each bowel movement. This treatment is not recommended for children under 12 years. The suppositories should not be used for more than two weeks unless advised otherwise by a doctor.

ANTHISAN CREAM

Use: A cream for the treatment and relief of itching and irritation caused by bites and stings, containing an antihistamine.

Dose: The cream should be applied to the affected area 2-3 times a day for up to three days. This treatment is not recommended for children under three years.

ANTHISAN PLUS STING RELIEF SPRAY

Use: A spray with a metered dose for the treatment and relief of itching and irritation caused by stings, rashes and bites. It contains an antihistamine and a mild anaesthetic.

Dose: To deliver a single dose, the nozzle head should be pressed once. Do this two or three times to the affected part. The spray can be used up to three times a day. This treatment is not recommended for children under three years.

ANUSOL OINTMENT AND CREAM

Use: Available in cream and ointment form for the treatment and relief of piles, containing bismuth, balsam of Peru and zinc oxide, all of which are astringents.

Dose: Should be applied at night and in the morning, and after each bowel movement. This treatment is not recommended for children under 12 years.

ANUSOL SUPPOSITORIES

Use: A suppository for the treatment and relief of piles, containing bismuth, balsam of Peru and zinc oxide.

Dose: One suppository should be inserted into the anus at night and one in the morning, and after each bowel movement. This treatment is not recommended for children under 12 years.

ANUSOL PLUS HC OINTMENT

Use: This is an ointment for the treatment and relief of piles, containing similar ingredients to those in the suppositories with the added ingredient of hydrocortisone, a steroid.

Dose: The ointment should be applied sparingly to the affected area at night and in the morning and after each bowel movement. This treatment is not recommended for children under 18 years. The ointment should not be used for more than seven days. The product is also available in suppository form.

AQUA-BAN
Use: Available in tablet form to relieve pre-menstrual water retention. It is a mild diuretic and contains caffeine.
Dose: Two tablets should be taken three times a day for the 4-5 days before a period is due. The tablets should not be taken for more than five days in one month.

ARRET
Use: Available in capsule form to stop diarrhoea. It contains loperamide.
Dose: Take two capsules initially and then one capsule after every loose bowel movement. Take a maximum of eight capsules over 24 hours. This treatment is not recommended for children under 12 years.

ASILONE ANTACID LIQUID
Use: A liquid remedy for the relief of indigestion, heartburn and upset stomach. It contains antacids, and dimethicone, an anti-flatulent.
Dose: 5-10 ml should be taken after meals and on retiring or as required. Take a maximum of 40 ml over 24 hours. This treatment is not recommended for children under 12 years.

ASILONE ANTACID TABLETS
Use: These tablets are for the relief of indigestion, heartburn, excess gas and an upset stomach, containing antacids.
Dose: 1-2 tablets should be taken before meals and at bedtime. This treatment is not recommended for children under 12 years.

ASKIT POWDERS
Use: An analgesic dissolvable powder which can be used for general pain relief. The powder contains 530mg of aspirin, aloxiprin and caffeine.
Dose: One sachet of powder should be mixed with water and taken every four hours. Take a maximum of six powders over 24 hours. This treatment is not recommended for children under 12 years.

ASPRO CLEAR
Use: These are effervescent analgesic tablets for the relief of general pain, containing 300 mg of aspirin.
Dose: 2-3 tablets should be dissolved in water every three hours. Take a maximum of 13 tablets over 24 hours. This treatment is not recommended for children under 12 years.

ATKINSON AND BARKER'S INFANT GRIPE MIXTURE

Use: A liquid remedy for the relief of colic and wind in infants, containing sodium bicarbonate, an antacid, dill and caraway oils.

Dose: 2.5-10 ml should be given every four hours depending on age. Always read the label. This treatment is not recommended for babies under one month.

AUDAX EAR DROPS

Use: These are drops for softening earwax. The drops contain a mild analgesic and an ingredient to soften the wax.

Dose: The ear should be filled with the liquid and plugged with cotton wool. Repeat this treatment twice a day for four days. This treatment is not recommended for children under one year.

AVOCA WART & VERRUCA SET

Use: This treatment is available as a kit for the removal of warts and verrucae. The kit contains a caustic pencil, an emery file, dressings and protector pads.

Dose: The pencil should be applied to the wart or verruca for one to two minutes and re-applied after 24 hours if required. Protect with the dressings provided. Use a maximum of three treatments for warts and six for verrucae.

AVOMINE

Use: Available in tablet form for the relief of travel sickness, containing promethazine, an antihistamine.

Dose: To prevent travel sickness, adults and children over 10 years should take one tablet on the night before a long journey or two hours before starting a shorter journey.

BABY MELTUS COUGH LINCTUS

Use: This is a liquid remedy for the treatment of coughs. It contains acetic acid, a soothing ingredient.

Dose: Babies (3-12 months) should be given 2.5 ml every two to three hours. Babies (13-30 months) should be given 5 ml every 2-3 hours. Babies over 30 months should be given 10 ml every 2-3 hours. This treatment is not recommended for babies under three months.

BALMOSA CREAM

Use: This is a cream rub for the relief of muscular aches and pains, containing rubefacients and a salicylate, an aspirin derivative.

Dose: The cream should be massaged into the affected area as required. This treatment is not recommended for children under six years.

BANSOR

Use: This treatment is available in liquid form for the treatment of bad breath and infections of the mouth and gums. It contains cetrimide, an anti-microbial.

Dose: To relieve sore gums apply a few drops to the affected area.

BAYER ASPIRIN

Use: Analgesic tablets which can be used for general pain relief, containing 300mg of aspirin.

Dose: 1-3 tablets should be taken every four hours. Take a maximum of 12 tablets over 24 hours. This treatment is not recommended for children under 12 years.

BAZUKA GEL

Use: A gel for the treatment of corns, calluses, warts and verrucae that comes an applicator and an emery board containing salicylic acid. The gel dries to form a water-resistant barrier over the affected area.

Dose: 1-2 drops should be applied to the corn or callus each night, then the area should be rubbed down once a week with the emery board. This treatment is not recommended for children under six years. The product is also available in Extra Strength form.

BECONASE ALLERGY

Use: Available in the form of a nasal spray for easing the congestion caused by hayfever. It contains beclomethasone, a steroid.

Dose: Two sprays should be applied into each nostril morning and evening. This treatment is not recommended for children under 12 years.

BEECHAMS ALL-IN-ONE

Use: This treatment is available in liquid form to alleviate the symptoms of colds and flu. It contains paracetamol, phenylephrine, a decongestant and guaiphenesin, an expectorant.

Dose: 20 ml should be taken up to twice a day. This treatment is not recommended for children under 12 years.

BEECHAMS FLU-PLUS CAPLETS

Use: Tablets for treatment of the symptoms of colds and flu, containing paracetamol, phenylephrine, a decongestant and caffeine.

Dose: Two capsules should be taken every 4-6 hours if required. Take a maximum of eight capsules over 24 hours. This treatment is not recommended for children under 12 years.

BEECHAMS FLU-PLUS HOT LEMON

Use: Available in the form of sachets of powder for relieving the symptoms of colds and flu. Each sachet contains paracetamol, phenylephrine, a decongestant and vitamin C.

Dose: One sachet should be dissolved in a mug of hot water every 4-6 hours. Take a maximum of four sachets over 24 hours. Treatment is not recommended for children under 12 years. Also available in other flavours.

BEECHAMS LEMON TABLETS

Use: Lemon flavoured tablets for the treatment of cold and flu symptoms, containing aspirin.

Dose: 1-2 tablets should be taken every 3-4 hours. Take a maximum of 12 tablets over 24 hours. This treatment is not recommended for children under 12 years.

BEECHAMS POWDERS

Use: These are sachets of powder that contain aspirin and caffeine for relieving the symptoms of colds and flu.

Dose: One sachet should be dissolved in hot water and taken every 3-4 hours. Take a maximum of six sachets over 24 hours. This treatment is not recommended for children under 12 years.

BEECHAMS POWDERS CAPSULES

Use: These are capsules for relieving the symptoms of colds and flu. They contain paracetamol, phenylephrine, a decongestant and caffeine.

Dose: Adults should take two capsules every 3-4 hours if required. Take a maximum of 12 capsules over 24 hours. Children (6-12 years) should take one capsule every three to four hours, with a maximum dose of six capsules in 24 hours. This treatment is not recommended for children under six years.

BEECHAMS WARMERS BLACKCURRANT

Use: Available in the form of sachets of powder for relieving the symptoms of colds and flu. Each sachet contains paracetamol, phenylephrine, a decongestant and vitamin C.

Dose: One sachet should be dissolved in hot water and taken every four hours. Take a maximum of six sachets over 24 hours. This treatment is not recommended for children under 12 years. The product is also available in other flavours.

BENADRYL ALLERGY RELIEF

Use: Available in capsule form for easing the symptoms of hayfever. Each capsule contains acrivastine, an antihistamine.

Dose: One capsule should be taken up to three times a day. This treatment is not recommended for children under 12 years, or for the elderly.

BENYLIN CHESTY COUGHS

Use: This is a liquid remedy for the treatment of coughs, containing diphenhydramine, an antihistamine and menthol.
Dose: Adults should take 10 ml four times a day. Children (6-12 years) should take 5 ml four times a day. This treatment is not recommended for children under six years. A non-drowsy version is also available.

BENYLIN CHILDREN'S CHESTY COUGHS

Use: A liquid remedy for the treatment of chesty coughs, containing guaiphenesin, an expectorant.
Dose: Children (6-12 years) should be given 10 ml four times a day, with a maximum of four doses a day. Children (1-5 years) should be given 5 ml four times a day, with a maximum of four doses a day. This treatment is not recommended for babies under one year.

BENYLIN CHILDREN'S COUGHS AND COLDS

Use: This is a sugar- and colour-free liquid remedy for treatment of the symptoms of coughs and colds. It contains dextromethorphan, a cough suppressant and triprolidine, an antihistamine.
Dose: Children (6-12 years) should take 10 ml 3-4 times a day. Children (2-5 years) should be given 5 ml 3-4 times a day. Children (1-2 years) should be given 2.5 ml 3-4 times a day. This treatment is not recommended for children under one year.

BENYLIN CHILDREN'S DRY COUGHS

Use: A liquid remedy for the treatment of dry coughs, containing pholcodine, a cough suppressant.
Dose: Children (6-12 years) should be given 10-15 ml three times a day. Children (1-5 years) should be given 5 ml three times a day. This treatment is not recommended for children under one year.

BENYLIN CHILDREN'S NIGHT COUGHS

Use: A liquid remedy for the treatment of coughs. It contains diphenhydramine, an antihistamine, and menthol.
Dose: Children (6 years and over) should take 10 ml no more than four times a day. Children (1-5 years) should take 5 ml no more than four times a day. This treatment is not recommended for children under one year.

BENYLIN COUGH AND CONGESTION

Use: A liquid remedy for the treatment of coughs, containing diphenhydramine, an antihistamine, dextromethorphan, a cough suppressant, pseudoephedrine, a decongestant and menthol.
Dose: Adults should take 10 ml no more than four times a day. Children (6-12 years) should take 5 ml no more than four times a day. This treatment is not recommended for children under six years.

BENYLIN DAY AND NIGHT COLD TREATMENT

Use: These are tablets for the treatment of colds and flu. The yellow tablets should be taken in the day and contain paracetamol and phenylpropanolamine, a decongestant. The blue night time tablets contain paracetamol and diphenhydramine, an antihistamine.

Dose: One yellow tablet should be taken three times a day and one blue tablet should be taken at night. This treatment is not recommended for children under six years.

BENYLIN DRY COUGHS

Use: A liquid remedy for the treatment of dry coughs, containing dextromethorphan, a cough suppressant, diphenhydramine, an antihistamine and menthol.

Dose: Adults should take 10 ml four times a day. Children (6-12 years) should take 5 ml four times a day. This treatment is not recommended for children under six years. A non-drowsy version is also available.

BENYLIN FOUR FLU LIQUID

Use: A liquid remedy for relieving the symptoms of colds and flu. The liquid contains pseudoephedrine, a decongestant, diphenhydramine, an antihistamine and paracetamol.

Dose: Adults should take 20 ml four times a day. Children (6-12 years) should take 10 ml four times a day. This treatment is not recommended for children under six years. Hot drink and tablet forms are also available.

BENYLIN WITH CODEINE

Use: A liquid remedy for the treatment of coughs, containing codeine, a cough suppressant and diphenhydramine, an antihistamine.

Dose: Adults should take 10 ml four times a day. Children (6-12 years) should be given 5 ml four times a day. This treatment is not recommended for children under six years.

BETACEPT ACNE WASH

Use: A liquid facial wash for the treatment of acne and spots, containing povidone iodine, an anti-microbial.

Dose: The wash should be used twice a day until the symptoms have disappeared. This treatment is not recommended for children under 15 years. Check the label for warnings about povidone iodine.

BETADINE SHAMPOO

Use: This is a medicated shampoo for the treatment of dandruff, containing povidone iodine, an anti-microbial.

Dose: Should be applied twice a week as an ordinary shampoo. Adults should use two to three capfuls. Children (2-12 years) should use 1-2 capfuls. This treatment is not recommended for children under two years.

BETADINE SKIN CLEANSER
Use: This is a liquid facial wash for the treatment of acne and spots. It contains povidone iodine, an anti-microbial.
Dose: The liquid should be applied with a damp sponge, lathered and left on for three to five minutes; then the skin should be rinsed with warm water and dried. Repeat this twice a day. This treatment is not recommended for children under two years. Read the label for warnings about povidone iodine.

BETADINE SPRAY
Use: A dry powder spray for the treatment of minor burns, scalds, cuts and grazes. It contains povidone iodine, an anti-microbial.
Dose: The spray should be applied onto the affected area once or twice a day as required, and covered with a clean dressing. This treatment is not recommended for children under two years.

BIORAL
Use: Available in the form of a gel for the treatment of mouth ulcers, containing carbenoxolone, which promotes healing of the ulcers.
Dose: The gel should be rubbed into the affected area after meals and at bedtime. The gel should be allowed to remain in contact with the ulcer for as long as possible. This treatment is not recommended for children.

BIRLEY'S ANTACID POWDER
Use: An antacid powder remedy for relieving the symptoms of indigestion and heartburn.
Dose: Adults should take 5 ml in water after each meal, or twice a day. Check the label for the correct dosage for children.

BISMAG
Use: Antacid tablets for relieving the symptoms of indigestion, heartburn and gastritis.
Dose: 2-4 tablets should be taken after meals. Repeat this dose after 15 minutes if required. Can also be taken on retiring. This treatment is not recommended for children under 12 years.

BISODOL ANTACID POWDER
Use: A remedy for indigestion and heartburn available in powder form, containing antacids and sodium.
Dose: 5 ml of the powder should be dissolved in water after meals. This treatment is not recommended for children. The product is also available in tablet form.

BISODOL HEARTBURN
Use: Tablets for relieving the symptoms of indigestion and heartburn,

containing antacids and sodium.
Dose: Adults should chew 1-2 tablets as required. Children (6-12 years) should chew one tablet after meals and at bedtime. This treatment is not recommended for children under six years.

BLISTEZE

Use: A cream for the treatment of cold sores. It contains ammonia, a soothing ingredient.
Dose: The cream should be applied to the affected area every two hours or as required.

BN LINIMENT

Use: A liniment for muscular aches and pains, containing rubefacients and a salicylate, an aspirin derivative.
Dose: The cream should be massaged into the affected part 2-3 times a day. For children over six years the liniment should be diluted with equal parts of olive oil before applying it to the affected part. This treatment is not recommended for children under six years.

BOCASAN

Use: A mouthwash available in powder form, for the treatment of bad breath and general mouth and gum infections. The powders contain sodium perborate – an anti-microbial, and a cleanser.
Dose: One sachet should be dissolved in water and used as a mouthwash three times a day after meals. Repeat this treatment for seven days. This treatment is not recommended for children under five years.

BONJELA

Use: A gel for the treatment of cold sores and mouth ulcers, containing choline salicylate, an aspirin derivative, and cetalkonium, an antiseptic.
Dose: A small quantity of the gel should be applied to the affected area every three hours. Use a maximum of six applications in 24 hours.

BONJELA ORAL PAIN-RELIEVING GEL

Use: A gel for easing teething pain in babies, containing choline salicylate – an analgesic, and an antiseptic.
Dose: The gel should be applied to the gums every three hours. Use a maximum of six applications over 24 hours. This treatment is not recommended for babies under four months.

BRADOSOL

Use: Lozenges for relieving sore throats, containing benzalkonium chloride, an antibacterial.
Dose: One lozenge should be sucked as required. This treatment is

not recommended for children under five years. Available in various flavours.

BRADOSOL PLUS

Use: Lozenges for relieving sore throats, containing domiphen bromide, an antibacterial, and lignocaine, an anaesthetic.

Dose: One lozenge should be sucked every 2-3 hours. Take a maximum of eight lozenges every 24 hours. This treatment is not recommended for children under 12 years.

BRASIVOL

Use: An abrasive paste used for the treatment of acne. It is available in two grades.

Dose: The affected area should be moistened, and the paste then rubbed in vigorously. Repeat this one to three times a day. The finer grade should be used first, and then the stronger grade progressed to if needed. This treatment is not recommended for children under 15 years.

BROLENE EYE DROPS

Use: Eye drops for the treatment of infections of the eye, containing propamidine, an anti-microbial.

Dose: 1-2 drops should be applied into the affected eye up to four times a day.

BROLENE EYE OINTMENT

Use: An ointment for the treatment of eye infections, including conjunctivitis and styes, containing dibromopropamidine, an anti-microbial.

Dose: The ointment should be applied to the infected eye/s twice a day.

BRONALIN DECONGESTANT

Use: A liquid remedy for the treatment of colds and flu, containing pseudoephedrine, a decongestant.

Dose: Adults should take 10 ml three times a day. Children (6-12 years) should be given 5 ml three times a day. Children (2-5 years) should be given 2.5 ml three times a day. This treatment is not recommended for children under two years.

BRONALIN DRY COUGH ELIXIR

Use: A liquid remedy for the treatment of coughs, containing dextromethorphan, a suppressant, and pseudoephedrine, a decongestant.

Dose: Adults should take 5-10 ml four times a day. Children (6-12 years) should be given 2.5 ml four times a day. This treatment is not recommended for children under six years.

BRONALIN EXPECTORANT LINCTUS

Use: A liquid remedy for the treatment of coughs, containing diphenhydramine, an antihistamine and sodium citrate and ammonium bicarbonate, both expectorants.

Dose: Adults should take 5-10 ml four times a day if required. Children (6-12 years) should take 5 ml four times a day if required. This treatment is not recommended for children under six years.

BRONALIN JUNIOR LINCTUS

Use: A liquid remedy for the treatment of coughs, containing diphenhydramine, an antihistamine and sodium citrate, an expectorant.
Dose: 5-10 ml, according to age, should be taken three times a day. Read the label for the correct dosage. This treatment is not recommended for children under one year.

BRULIDINE CREAM

Use: A white cream for the treatment of minor burns and scalds, nappy rash and other minor skin infections. Contains dibromopropamidine isethionate 0.15%.
Dose: After cleaning wound, apply direct or on lint. Renew two or three times daily.

BRUSH OFF COLD SORE LOTION

Use: A lotion treatment for cold sores, containing povidone iodine, an antiseptic.
Dose: The lotion should be applied twice a day.

BURNEZE

Use: A spray for the treatment of minor burns and scalds. It contains benzocaine, an anaesthetic.
Dose: The spray should be applied onto the affected area and then again after 15 minutes if required.

BUSCOPAN TABLETS

Use: Tablets containing an antispasmodic, for relieving period pains.
Dose: Two tablets should be taken up to four times a day when necessary.

BUTTERCUP SYRUP (ORIGINAL)

Use: A liquid remedy for relieving coughs, containing capsicum and squill, both expectorants.
Dose: Adults should take 10 ml three times a day. Children over two years should be given 5 ml. This treatment is not recommended for children under two years. The product is also available in honey and lemon flavour.

BUTTERCUP INFANT COUGH SYRUP
Use: A liquid remedy for relieving coughs, containing ipecacuanha, an expectorant, menthol and liquid glucose.
Dose: Children (1-5 years) should be given 5 ml 3-4 times a day. This treatment is not recommended for children under one year.

CABDRIVER'S COUGH LINCTUS
Use: A liquid remedy for the treatment of coughs, containing dextromethorphan – a cough suppressant – terpin, menthol, pumilio pine oil and eucalyptus oil.
Dose: 5 ml should be taken every four hours. This treatment is not recommended for children under 12 years.

CALADRYL CREAM
Use: A cream containing an antihistamine for relieving bites, stings, rashes and sunburn.
Dose: The cream should be applied to the affected part 2-3 times a day as required. The product is also available as a lotion.

CALGEL TEETHING GEL
Use: A gel for relieving teething pains in babies, containing lignocaine – an anaesthetic – and an antiseptic.
Dose: The cream should be applied up to six times a day, leaving a minimum of 20 minutes between applications. This treatment is not recommended for babies under three months.

CALIFIG CALIFORNIA SYRUP OF FIGS
Use: A liquid remedy for the treatment of constipation, containing senna, a stimulant laxative.
Dose: 7.5-30 ml (depending on age) should be taken on retiring. Read the label for the correct dosage. This treatment is not recommended for children under one year.

CALIMAL ANTIHISTAMINE TABLETS
Use: Tablets for relieving the symptoms of hayfever, containing chlorpheniramine, an antihistamine.
Dose: Adults should take one tablet 3-4 times a day. Children (6-12 years) should take half to one tablet 3-4 times a day. This treatment is not recommended for children under six years.

CALPOL INFANT SUSPENSION
Use: A strawberry flavoured analgesic liquid for general pain relief, containing 120 mg of paracetamol in every 5 ml.
Dose: A maximum of four doses can be taken over 24 hours. Babies (3-12 months) should be given 2.5 ml every four hours if required, with no more than 20 ml in 24 hours. Children (1-5 years) should be given

5-10 ml every four hours. This treatment is not recommended for babies under three months.

CALPOL SIX PLUS SUSPENSION
Use: A strawberry flavoured analgesic for general pain relief that is sugar- and colour-free, containing 250 mg of paracetamol in every 5 ml.
Dose: A maximum of four doses can be taken in 24 hours. Children (6-12 years) should be given 5-10 ml every four hours if required. For children under six years use Calpol Infant Suspension.

CAM
Use: A liquid symptomatic treatment of bronchospasm in children and adults with bronchitis. Contains ephedrine hydrochloride.
Dose: Adults and children over 12 years should take four 5 ml spoonfuls three times a day, if necessary. Children (4-12 years) should take two 5 ml spoonfuls three times a day. Children (6 months to 2 years) should take 2.5 ml (using a measuring dropper) three times a day. Do not give to infants under 6 months. Avoid in hypertension, hyperthyroidism, cardiovascular problems, hyperexcitability, glaucoma, prostatic enlargement, phaechromocytoma. Not to be used by patients taking MAOIa or within 14 days of stopping MAOI treatment.

CANESTEN 1% CREAM
Use: A cream treatment for the treatment of nappy rash, containing clotrimazole, an antifungal.
Dose: The cream should be massaged gently into clean, dry skin 2-3 times a day.

CANESTEN AF CREAM
Use: An antifungal cream containing clotrimazole for the treatment of athlete's foot.
Dose: The cream should be rubbed gently into the affected area 2-3 times a day, and should be used for four weeks.

CANESTEN AF POWDER
Use: A powder treatment for athlete's foot, containing clotrimazole.
Dose: The powder should be sprinkled onto the affected area 2-3 times a day. It is also advisable to dust the inside of socks and footwear each day. This treatment may be continued for four weeks.

CANESTEN AF SPRAY
Use: A spray treatment for athlete's foot, containing clotrimazole, an antifungal ingredient.
Dose: The feet should be washed and dried, particularly between the toes. The product should then be sprayed thinly all over the affected

area 2-3 times a day. The treatment should be continued for one month.

CANESTEN COMBI

Use: A combination treatment for thrush comprising of a cream containing 1 per cent clotrimazole – an antifungal drug – and one pessary containing 500 mg of clotrimazole. An applicator is included in the pack.

Dose: One pessary should be inserted into the vagina at night. The cream should be applied twice daily to the external area around the vagina and also applied to the partner's penis.

CANESTEN HYDROCORTISONE

Use: A cream for the treatment of athlete's foot, containing clotrimazole – an antifungal – and a steroid.

Dose: The cream should be applied thinly to the affected area and rubbed in gently. The product should not be used for more than seven days.

CANESTEN 1 PESSARY

Use: A pessary for the treatment of thrush, containing 500 mg of clotrimazole, an antifungal drug. An applicator is included in the pack.

Dose: The pessary should be inserted into the vagina at night. This is a single-dose treatment.

CANESTEN 10% VAGINAL CREAM

Use: A cream for the treatment of thrush, containing 10 per cent clotrimazole, an antifungal drug. An applicator is included in the pack.

Dose: The cream should be applied once into the vagina.

CAPASAL SHAMPOO

Use: A shampoo remedy for the treatment of cradle cap in children, containing coal tar, coconut oil and salicylic acid.

Dose: Shampoo the baby's head, rinse and repeat. The treatment can be applied once daily if necessary.

CAPASAL THERAPEUTIC SHAMPOO

Use: A medicated shampoo for the treatment of dandruff, containing coal tar, salicylic acid and coconut oil.

Dose: Should be used as a shampoo when required.

CAPRIN

Use: Analgesic tablets which can be used for general pain relief, containing 300 mg of aspirin.

Dose: 1-3 tablets should be taken 3-4 times a day. Take a maximum of 12 tablets over 24 hours. This treatment is not recommended for children under 12 years.

CARBALAX

Use: Suppository for the treatment of constipation. Suppositories contain sodium bicarbonate 1.08g, anhydrous sodium acid phosphate 1.32g equivalent to sodium acid phosphate 1.69g.
Dose: Insert one into the rectum 30 minutes before evacuation required. Not recommended for children.

CARBELLON

Use: Antacid tablets for relieving indigestion, heartburn and gastritis.
Dose: Adults should take 2-4 tablets three times a day. Children over six years should be given two tablets three times a day. This treatment is not recommended for children under six years.

CARNATION CALLUS CAPS

Use: A medicated plaster containing salicylic acid for the treatment of corns and calluses.
Dose: The plaster should be applied to the affected area and changed after three days. The callus can be removed after six days. This treatment is not recommended for children under 16 years.

CARNATION CORN CAPS

Use: Medicated plasters for the treatment of corns, containing salicylic acid.
Dose: The plaster should be applied and changed every two days. The corn can be removed after six days. This treatment is not recommended for children under 15 years unless advised otherwise by a doctor. Do not use for more than 10 days, and do not use more than five caps in that time.

CARNATION VERRUCA CARE

Use: Medicated pads used for the removal of verrucae, containing salicylic acid.
Dose: The pad should be applied and changed every two days, for up to 10 days. The treatment can be repeated after a month. This treatment is not recommended for children under six years, unless advised otherwise by a doctor.

CATARRH-EX

Use: Capsules for relieving catarrh, containing phenylephrine, a decongestant, paracetamol and caffeine.
Dose: 1-2 capsules should be taken every 4-6 hours. Take a maximum of eight capsules in 24 hours.

CEANEL CONCENTRATE
Use: A medicated shampoo for the treatment of dandruff, containing various anti-microbials.
Dose: Should be used as a shampoo three times a week for one week, then twice a week as required.

CEPTON
Use: A wash for the treatment of acne, containing chlorhexidine, an anti-microbial.
Dose: The wash should be applied to clean skin and left for one minute before rinsing off thoroughly. This treatment is not recommended for children under 15 years. The product is also available in the form of a lotion.

CERUMOL EAR DROPS
Use: Ear drops for removing earwax, containing a mild analgesic and an ingredient for softening the wax.
Dose: Five drops should be applied into the affected ear and left for 20 minutes. This should be repeated two to three times a day for three days.

CETAVLEX
Use: A cream for the treatment of minor burns, scalds, cuts and grazes, containing cetrimide, an antiseptic.
Dose: The cream should be applied to the affected area as required.

CETRIMIDE CREAM
Use: An antiseptic cream for the treatment of minor wounds or irritations of the skin, containing cetrimide.
Dose: The cream should be applied to the affected area or smeared on a dressing to cover the wound.

CLARITEYES
Use: Eye drops for relieving irritated eyes caused by hayfever. They contain sodium cromoglycate, an anti-inflammatory.
Dose: 1-2 drops should be applied to each affected eye up to four times a day. This treatment is not recommended for children under five years.

CLARITYN ALLERGY
Use: Tablets for relieving the symptoms of hayfever, containing loratadine, an antihistamine.
Dose: One tablet should be taken daily. This treatment is not recommended for children under 12 years.

CLARITYN ALLERGY SYRUP

Use: A liquid remedy for relieving the symptoms of hayfever. It contains loratadine, an antihistamine.

Dose: Adults should take 10 ml once a day. Children (2-5 years) should be given half the adult dose. This treatment is not recommended for children under two years.

CLEARASIL

Use: A cream for the treatment of acne and spots, containing benzoyl peroxide.

Dose: The cream should be applied once a day for one week. Increase applications to twice a day after one week if there are no adverse effects. This treatment is not recommended for children under 12 years.

CLEARASIL TREATMENT CREAM (REGULAR)

Use: A cream treatment for acne and spots, containing triclosan, an anti-microbial, and sulphur.

Dose: The cream should be applied twice daily to clean skin. This treatment is not recommended for children under 15 years.

CLINITAR CREAM

Use: A cream for the treatment of dermatitis and eczema, containing coal tar.

Dose: The cream should be applied once or twice a day as required.

CLINITAR SHAMPOO

Use: A medicated shampoo for the treatment of dandruff, containing coal tar.

Dose: The shampoo should be used up to three times a week

COCOIS SCALP OINTMENT

Use: An ointment for the treatment of dandruff, containing coal tar.

Dose: The ointment should be applied to the scalp once a week as necessary. For severe conditions apply daily for three to seven days. Shampoo the hair one hour after using the ointment. This treatment is not recommended for children under six years.

CODIS 500

Use: A soluble analgesic tablet that can be used for general pain relief. Each tablet contains 500 mg of aspirin and 8 mg of codeine phosphate.

Dose: 1-2 tablets should be dissolved in water and taken every four hours as required. Take a maximum of eight tablets over 24 hours. This treatment is not recommended for children under 12 years.

COJENE
Use: Analgesic tablets which can be used for general pain relief, containing 300 mg of aspirin, 8 mg of codeine phosphate and caffeine.
Dose: 1-2 tablets should be taken every four hours. Take a maximum of six tablets in 24 hours. This treatment is not recommended for children under 12 years.

COLOFAC IBS
Use: A tablet remedy for easing the symptoms of irritable bowel syndrome. The tablets contain mebeverine, an ingredient that helps to calm intestinal spasms.
Dose: One tablet should be taken three times a day, preferably 20 minutes before meals. This treatment is not recommended for children under 10 years.

COLPERMIN
Use: Capsules for irritable bowel syndrome, containing peppermint oil for calming intestinal spasms.
Dose: 1-2 capsules should be taken three times a day for up to two weeks. The capsules should be swallowed whole to prevent the peppermint oil irritating the throat. This treatment is not recommended for children under 15 years.

COLSOR
Use: A cream treatment for cold sores, containing tannic acid and phenol, astringents, and menthol, a soothing ingredient.
Dose: The cream should be applied as required. The product is also available in the form of a lotion.

COMPOUND W
Use: A liquid treatment for warts and verrucae, containing salicylic acid.
Dose: The liquid should be applied to the wart or verruca daily for up to 12 weeks. This treatment is not recommended for children under six years.

CONOTRANE CREAM
Use: A cream for the treatment of nappy rash, containing benzalkonium chloride – an antiseptic – and dimethicone, a soothing agent.
Dose: The cream should be applied after every nappy change.

CONTAC 400
Use: Capsules for relieving the symptoms of colds and flu, containing chlorpheniramine, an antihistamine, and phenylpropanolamine, a decongestant.

Dose: One capsule should be taken in the morning and another before retiring. This treatment is not recommended for children under 12 years.

COPHOLCO

Use: A liquid remedy for the treatment of coughs, containing pholcodine, a cough suppressant, terpin, menthol and cineole.

Dose: Adults should take 10 ml four to five times a day. Children over eight years should be given 5 ml per day. This treatment is not recommended for children under eight years.

CORLAN

Use: A tablet for the treatment of mouth ulcers, containing hydrocortisone, a corticosteroid.

Dose: One tablet should be dissolved near the site of the ulcer four times a day. This treatment is not recommended for children under 12 years, unless advised otherwise by a doctor.

CORSODYL

Use: This is a mouthwash for the treatment of mouth infections, sore gums and bad breath. It contains chlorhexidine, an anti-microbial.

Dose: The mouth should be rinsed with 10 ml of the mouthwash for one minute. This should be carried out daily for one month.

CORSODYL DENTAL GEL

Use: A gel for the treatment of mouth infections such as thrush and mouth ulcers, containing chlorhexidine, an antiseptic.

Dose: The gel should be applied directly onto the affected area once or twice a day and left for one minute.

COVONIA BRONCHIAL BALSAM

Use: A liquid remedy for the treatment of coughs, containing dextromethorphan – a cough suppressant – and menthol.

Dose: Adults should take 10 ml every four hours. Children (6-12 years) should be given 5 ml every four hours. This treatment is not recommended for children under six years. The elderly should check with their doctor or pharmacist prior to use.

COVONIA FOR CHILDREN

Use: A liquid remedy for the treatment of coughs, containing dextromethorphan – a cough suppressant – and benzoic acid.

Dose: Children should be given 5-10 ml according to age, every four to six hours as required. Read the label for the correct dosage. This treatment is not recommended for children under two years.

COVONIA MENTHOLATED COUGH MIXTURE

Use: A liquid remedy for the treatment of coughs, containing squill and liquorice – both expectorants – and menthol.
Dose: Adults should take 5-10 ml every four hours. Children (5-12 years) should be given 5 ml every four hours. This treatment is not recommended for children under five years.

COVONIA NIGHT TIME FORMULA

Use: A liquid remedy for the treatment of coughs, containing dextromethorphan, a cough suppressant, and diphenhydramine, an antihistamine.
Dose: 15 ml should be taken before retiring. This treatment is not recommended for children under five years.

CRAMPEX

Use: This is a tablet remedy for dispelling cramps, containing nicotinic acid, which improves the circulation.
Dose: 1-2 tablets should be taken before bedtime. This treatment is not recommended for children.

CREMALGIN

Use: A cream rub for relieving muscular aches and pains, containing rubefacients and a salicylate, an aspirin derivative.
Dose: The cream should be massaged into the affected area twice or three times a day. This treatment is not recommended for children under six years.

CULLENS HEADACHE POWDERS

Use: Analgesic powder for the treatment of headache. Sachets contain aspirin 600 mg, caffeine 62 mg and calcium phosphate 34.08 mg.
Dose: One powder repeated every 3-4 hours as necessary. Do not exceed six doses in 24 hours. Do not take if you have a stomach ulcer. Not to be taken by children under 12 years.

CUPAL BABY CHEST RUB

Use: An aromatic ointment for relieving catarrh and congestion in young children and babies over three months. The ointment contains eucalyptus and menthol oils.
Dose: The ointment should be rubbed gently into the chest, throat and back twice a day.

CUPLEX

Use: A gel containing salicylic acid for the treatment of calluses, corns, warts and verrucae.
Dose: This gel should be applied at night to the affected part. When it is dry, Cuplex produces a protective film, which should be removed

in the mornings. This treatment may take between six and twelve weeks before it shows a result. The product is not recommended for young children.

CUPROFEN
Use: Analgesic tablets which can be used for general pain relief, containing 200 mg of ibuprofen.
Dose: Two tablets should be taken after food. 1-2 tablets can be taken every four hours if required. Take a maximum of six tablets in 24 hours. This treatment is not recommended for children under 12 years.

CUPROFEN IBUTOP GEL
Use: A gel containing ibuprofen for relieving muscular aches and pains, which is non-steroidal anti-inflammatory (NSAID).
Dose: The gel should be applied to the affected area, allowing at least four hours between applications. Do not use more than four times in 24 hours. This treatment is not recommended for children under 12 years.

CUPROFEN MAXIMUM STRENGTH
Use: Analgesic tablets which can be used for general pain relief, containing 400 mg of ibuprofen.
Dose: One tablet should be taken with food every eight hours. Take a maximum of three tablets in 24 hours. This treatment is not recommended for children under 12 years.

CURASH
Use: A powder treatment for nappy rash, containing zinc oxide, an antiseptic and an astringent.
Dose: The powder should be applied after every nappy change. Try to avoid inhalation by baby and do not apply to broken skin.

CYMALON
Use: Granules containing sodium citrate and sodium bicarbonate for relieving the symptoms of cystitis.
Dose: One sachet of the granules should be dissolved in water, and taken three times a day for two days.

CYMEX
Use: A cream treatment for cold sores, which contains cetrimide, an antiseptic, and urea, a soothing ingredient.
Dose: The cream should be applied sparingly every hour if necessary.

CYSTOLEVE
Use: Sachets of granules for the treatment of cystitis, containing sodium nitrate.

Dose: One sachet of granules should be dissolved in water three times a day for two days.

CYSTOPURIN
Use: Sachets of granules for the treatment of cystitis, containing potassium citrate.
Dose: One sachet of granules should be dissolved in water three times a day for two days.

DAKTARIN DUAL ACTION CREAM
Use: A cream for the treatment of athlete's foot, containing the antifungal ingredient, miconazole.
Dose: The cream should be applied twice a day to the affected area. Continue this treatment for a further 10 days after the infection has cleared up.

DAKTARIN DUAL ACTION POWDER
Use: A spray-on treatment for athlete's foot. The powder contains miconazole, an antifungal ingredient.
Dose: The powder should be applied to the affected area twice a day. Continue with this treatment for a further 10 days after the infection has cleared up.

DAKTARIN ORAL GEL
Use: A gel treatment for oral thrush, containing miconazole, an antifungal.
Dose: A small amount of the gel should be applied and held in the mouth for as long as possible and then spat out. Repeat this four times a day. The dosage for children varies according to age. Always read the label. Continue treatment for a further two days after the infection has cleared up.

DAYLEVE
Use: A cream for the treatment of stings, bites, hives, eczema and dermatitis. It contains hydrocortisone, a steroid.
Dose: The cream should be applied thinly to the affected area twice a day. This treatment is not recommended for children under 10 years.

DAY NURSE
Use: A liquid remedy for relieving the symptoms of colds and flu, containing paracetamol, phenylpropanolamine, a decongestant and dextromethorphan, a cough suppressant.
Dose: Adults should take 20 ml every four hours. Take a maximum of 80 ml over 24 hours. Children (6-12 years) should be given 10 ml every four hours. This treatment is not recommended for children under six years. The product is also available in capsule form and as a hot drink.

DDD MEDICATED CREAM

Use: A medicated antiseptic cream that is used for the treatment of minor wounds and skin irritations. It contains thymol, menthol, salicylic acid, chlorbutol and titanium dioxide.

Dose: The cream should be applied morning and evening until the problem has cleared up.

DDD MEDICATED LOTION

Use: A medicated antiseptic lotion that can be used for the treatment of minor wounds and skin irritations, containing thymol, menthol, salicylic acid, chlorobutol, methyl salicylate, glycerin and ethanol.

Dose: The cream should be applied to the affected area as needed.

DECUBAL CLINIC CREAM

Use: Emollient and moisturiser for dry and scaly skin conditions including dermatitis, ichthyosis, hyperkeratosis, and psoriasis. Cream contains isopropyl myristate, glycerol, anhydrous lanolin and dimethicone.

Dose: Apply two to three times daily. Should not be used on open wounds, but can be used on cracked skin associated with dry skin conditions. Avoid eye area. For external use only.

DEEP FREEZE

Use: A cooling spray treatment for relieving muscular aches.

Dose: The treatment should be sprayed onto the affected area as required but no more than three times in 24 hours. This treatment is not recommended for children under six years.

DEEP FREEZE COOLING GEL

Use: A gel for soothing muscular aches which contains cooling ingredients.

Dose: The gel should be rubbed into the affected area 3-4 times a day. This treatment is not recommended for children under five years.

DEEP HEAT MASSAGE LINIMENT

Use: A liniment for the treatment of muscular aches and pains, containing rubefacients and a salicylate, an aspirin derivative.

Dose: The cream should be rubbed into the affected area 3-4 times a day. This treatment is not recommended for children under five years.

DEEP HEAT MAXIMUM STRENGTH

Use: A cream for relieving muscular aches and pains, containing a rubefacient and a salicylate, an aspirin derivative.

Dose: The product should be massaged into the affected area 2-3 times a day. This treatment is not recommended for children under five years.

DEEP HEAT RUB

Use: A cream rub treatment for relieving muscular aches and pains, containing rubefacients, and a salicylate, an aspirin derivative.
Dose: The product should be massaged into the affected area 2-3 times a day. This treatment is not recommended for children under six years.

DEEP HEAT SPRAY

Use: A spray for easing muscular aches and pains, containing rubefacients and a salicylate, an aspirin derivative.
Dose: The affected area should be sprayed with 2-3 short bursts as required. This treatment is not recommended for children under six years.

DEEP RELIEF

Use: A gel treatment for relieving muscular aches and pains, containing ibuprofen, a non-steroidal anti-inflammatory (NSAID).
Dose: The gel should be massaged into the affected area up to three times a day. This treatment is not recommended for children under 12 years.

DENOREX ANTI-DANDRUFF SHAMPOO

Use: A medicated shampoo for the treatment of dandruff, containing coal tar.
Dose: Should be used as a shampoo on alternate days. Continue this treatment for 10 days, then use 2-3 times a week if required. The product is also available as a shampoo with conditioner.

DENTINOX CRADLE CAP TREATMENT SHAMPOO

Use: A shampoo for the treatment of cradle cap.
Dose: The treatment should be used as a normal shampoo at every bath time until the condition clears up.

DENTINOX INFANT COLIC DROPS

Use: A liquid remedy for relieving colic in infants, containing dimethicone, an anti-wind ingredient.
Dose: 2.5 ml should be given with or after each feed. A maximum of six doses can be given in one day. The product can be used from birth onwards.

DENTINOX TEETHING GEL

Use: A gel for soothing teething pain in babies, containing an antiseptic and lignocaine, an anaesthetic.
Dose: The gel should be applied every 20 minutes as required and is suitable for use from birth onwards.

DENTOGEN
Use: A gel for relieving toothache, containing clove oil.
Dose: The gel should be rubbed onto the affected tooth.

DEQUACAINE LOZENGES
Use: Lozenges for relieving sore throats, containing dequalinium, an antibacterial, and benzocaine, an anaesthetic.
Dose: One lozenge should be dissolved in the mouth every two hours or as required. Take a maximum of eight lozenges in 24 hours. This treatment is not recommended for children under 12 years.

DEQUADIN
Use: Orange coloured lozenges, each containing dequalinium chloride for the symptomatic relief of sore throats, glossitis, pharyngitis, mouth ulcers and oral thrush.
Dose: Adults and children over 12 should suck one lozenge every 2-3 hours, up to a maximum of eight in 24 hours..

DERBAC M LIQUID
Use: A liquid treatment for head lice and other similar infestations, containing malathion.
Dose: For head lice, the liquid should be applied to the affected area, combed through the hair while wet, left to dry and finally washed out after 12 hours. For pubic lice, it should be left on for 1-12 hours, or longer if possible. For scabies, it should be applied to the whole body and left for 24 hours before washing off. This treatment is not recommended for babies under six months.

DERMACORT CREAM
Use: A cream for the treatment of bites, stings, hives, eczema and dermatitis, containing hydrocortisone, a steroid.
Dose: The product should be applied to the affected area once or twice a day. This treatment is not recommended for children under 10 years.

DERMAMIST
Use: An emollient spray for the treatment of eczema and dermatitis, containing a mixture of oils.
Dose: The product should be sprayed onto the affected areas after a bath or shower.

DERMIDEX CREAM
Use: A cream for the treatment of bites, stings, eczema, dermatitis and hives, containing an anaesthetic and antiseptic.
Dose: The product should be applied to the affected part every three hours if necessary. Treatment is not recommended for children under four years.

DETTOL ANTISEPTIC PAIN RELIEF SPRAY

Use: A liquid antiseptic spray with a mild anaesthetic for the treatment of minor wounds and skin irritations, containing benzalkonium chloride and lidocaine hydrochloride.

Dose: The liquid should be sprayed onto the affected area as required.

DETTOL CREAM

Use: An antiseptic cream for the treatment of minor wounds or irritations of the skin, containing triclosan, chloro-xylenol and edetic acid.

Dose: The cream should be applied thinly onto the affected area.

DETTOL FRESH

Use: A liquid antiseptic and disinfectant for the treatment of minor wounds and irritations of the skin, containing benzalkonium chloride.

Dose: 50 ml should be diluted in 1 litre of water and applied to the affected area.

DETTOL LIQUID

Use: A liquid antiseptic and disinfectant for the treatment of minor wounds and irritations of the skin, containing chloroxyenol.

Dose: The liquid should be diluted with water as appropriate for its intended use.

DE WITT'S ANTACID POWDER

Use: An antacid powder for relieving indigestion and heartburn, containing sodium.

Dose: 1 teaspoon of the powder should be dissolved in water and taken after meals. This treatment is not recommended for children under 12 years. The product is also available in tablet form.

DE WITT'S THROAT LOZENGES

Use: Lozenges for relieving sore throats, containing cetylp yearidium chloride, an antibacterial.

Dose: Adults should take one lozenge every three hours. Take a maximum of eight in 24 hours. Children over six years should be given half the adult dose with a maximum of four in 24 hours. This treatment is not recommended for children under six years.

DE WITT'S WORM SYRUP

Use: A liquid remedy for removing intestinal worms. The liquid contains piperazine citrate, an anti-worm ingredient.

Dose: For threadworms, adults should take 15 ml daily for seven days. Children should be given 5-10 ml, according to age. For roundworms, adults should take one dose of 3 ml. Children should be given one dose of 10-25 ml, according to age. This treatment is not recommended for children under two years.

DIASORB
Use: Capsules for the treatment of diarrhoea, containing loperamide.
Dose: Two capsules should be taken initially, then one capsule after each loose bowel movement. Take a maximum of eight capsules in 24 hours. This treatment is not recommended for children under 12 years.

DIFFLAM
Use: A cream for relieving muscular aches and pains, containing benzydamine, a non-steroidal anti-inflammatory (NSAID).
Dose: The cream should be massaged into the affected area three times a day. This treatment is not recommended for children under six years.

DIFLUCAN
Use: An oral capsule for the treatment of thrush, containing 150 mg of fluconazole.
Dose: One capsule should be taken orally. This is a single-dose treatment.

DIJEX
Use: A liquid remedy for relieving indigestion, heartburn and general digestive discomfort, containing an antacid.
Dose: Adults should take 5-10 ml four times a day and on retiring. Children over six years should be given 5 ml three times a day. This treatment is not recommended for children under six years.

DIMOTANE CO
Use: A liquid remedy for the treatment of coughs, containing brompheniramine, an antihistamine, pseudoephedrine, a decongestant, codeine, a cough suppressant and ethanol (alcohol).
Dose: Adults should take 5-10 ml up to four times a day. Children (4-12 years) should be given 5-7.5 ml three times a day, depending on age. Read the label for the correct dosage. This treatment is not recommended for children under four years. The product is also available in a children's formula.

DIMOTAPP ELIXIR
Use: A liquid remedy for the treatment of colds and flu, containing brompheniramine, an antihistamine and phenylephrine, a decongestant.
Dose: Adults should take 5-10 ml three times a day. Children (6-12 years) should be given 5 ml three times a day. Children (2-6 years) should be given 2.5 ml three times a day. This treatment is not recommended for children under two years. Tablet and children's versions are also available.

DINNEFORDS TEEJEL GEL
Use: A gel for relieving teething pains in babies, containing choline

salicylate, an analgesic and an antiseptic.

Dose: 2 cm of the gel should be applied to the gums every 3-4 hours as required. This treatment is not recommended for babies under four months.

DIOCALM DUAL ACTION

Use: A tablet remedy for stopping diarrhoea, containing morphine and attapulgite.

Dose: Two tablets should be taken every two to four hours as required. Take a maximum of 12 tablets in 24 hours. Children (6-12 years) should be given one tablet every 2-4 hours, with a maximum of six tablets in 24 hours. This treatment is not recommended for children under six years.

DIOCALM REPLENISH

Use: A powder remedy to stop diarrhoea. It also aids recovery after diarrhoea by replacing the water and salts lost from the body.

Dose: Adults should take 1-2 sachets dissolved in a measured amount of water, as stated on the packet, after every loose bowel movement. Children (6-12 years) should be given one sachet dissolved in water at the start of diarrhoea, with a repeat dose after every bowel movement. Take a maximum of nine sachets in 24 hours. For bottle-fed babies, use the equivalent volume as a substitute for a bottle-feed. Milk should be gradually re-introduced after 24 hours. Discuss with a doctor before giving medication to babies under 12 months.

DIOCALM ULTRA

Use: Capsules for stopping diarrhoea, containing loperamide.

Dose: Two capsules should be taken at the start of the diarrhoea, followed by one capsule after every loose bowel movement. Take a maximum of eight capsules in 24 hours. This treatment is not recommended for children under 12 years.

DIOCTYL

Use: Capsules for easing constipation, containing docusate, a stimulant laxative with a stool-softening action.

Dose: Adults can take up to five capsules through the day. The dosage should be reduced as the condition improves. This treatment is not recommended for children under 12 years. The product is also available as a solution and in a lower dose form for children.

DIORALYTE NATURAL

Use: A powder remedy to help replace the salts and water lost during an attack of diarrhoea.

Dose: Adults should take 1-2 sachets of the powder in a measured amount of water after each loose bowel movement. Children should be given one sachet. Bottle-fed infants should be given a diluted solution instead of their feed – read the instructions on the packet for the correct dosage. Always consult a doctor before giving this treatment to babies under one year. This product is also available in other flavours.

DIORALYTE RELIEF
Use: A powder formula to replace salts and water lost from the body during an attack of diarrhoea.
Dose: One sachet should be dissolved in a measured quantity of water. Read the instructions on the packet. Take a maximum of five sachets in 24 hours. The product can be taken up to 3-4 days after loose bowel movements. Consult a doctor before giving the solution to babies under one year.

DIPROBASE
Use: An emollient cream for relieving the discomfort of eczema and dermatitis, containing a mixture of oils.
Dose: The cream should be applied when necessary.

DIPROBATH
Use: An emollient bath additive for relieving the discomfort of eczema and dermatitis, containing oil.
Dose: The liquid should be added to bathwater.

DISPRIN
Use: A soluble analgesic tablet which can be used for general pain relief, containing 300 mg of aspirin.
Dose: 2-3 tablets should be taken every four hours. Take a maximum of 13 tablets in 24 hours. The treatment is not recommended for children under 12 years.

DISPRIN DIRECT
Use: Analgesic tablets which can be used for general pain relief and can be dissolved in the mouth without water. Each tablet contains 300mg of aspirin.
Dose: 1-3 tablets should be taken every four hours as required. Take a maximum of 13 tablets in 24 hours. This treatment is not recommended for children under 12 years.

DISPRIN EXTRA
Use: A soluble analgesic tablet which can be used for general pain relief, containing 300 mg of aspirin and 200 mg of paracetamol.
Dose: 1-2 tablets should be dissolved in water every four hours as required. Take a maximum of six tablets in 24 hours. This treatment is not recommended for children under 12 years.

DISPROL PARACETAMOL SUSPENSION

Use: A banana-flavoured, sugar-free analgesic liquid which can be used for general pain relief, containing 120mg of paracetamol in every 5 ml.
Dose: Babies (3-12 months) should be given 2.5-5 ml every four hours if required, with a maximum of four doses in 24 hours. Children (1-6 years) should be given 5-10 ml every four hours if required, with a maximum of four doses in 24 hours. The treatment is not recommended for babies under three months.

DOAN'S

Use: Analgesic tablets for the treatment of mild to moderate pain. The tablets contain paracetamol and sodium salicylate.
Dose: Adults should take 2-3 tablets every 4 hours to a maximum of 16 in a 24 hour period. This treatment is not to be given to children under 12 years.

DOCUSOL ADULT SOLUTION

Use: Liquid medicine to prevent and treat constipation. Liquid contains docusate sodium 50 mg in 5 ml.
Dose: Adults should take up to 50ml per day in divided doses. Do not take if there is abdominal pain, nausea or vomiting.

DOCUSOL PAEDIATRIC SOLUTION

Use: Liquid medicine to prevent and treat constipation. Liquid contains docusate sodium 12.5 mg in 5 ml.
Dose: Children over 2 years should take 5 10ml spoonfuls up to three times a day. Children 6 months to 2 years should take 5ml up to three times daily. Do not take if there is abdominal pain, nausea or vomiting.

DO-DO CHESTEZE

Use: Tablets for the treatment of coughs, containing ephedrine, a decongestant, theophylline, a bronchodilator, and caffeine.
Dose: Adults should take no more than one tablet in four hours. Take a maximum of four tablets in 24 hours. Children over 12 years should be given a maximum of three tablets in 24 hours. This treatment is not recommended for children under 12 years.

DO-DO CHESTEZE EXPECTORANT SYRUP

Use: A liquid remedy for the treatment of coughs, containing guaiphenesin, an expectorant.
Dose: 5-10 ml should be taken every two to four hours. This treatment is not recommended for children under 12 years.

DOLVAN TABLETS

Use: Tablets for the treatment of colds and flu, containing paracetamol, diphenhydramine, an antihistamine, ephedrine, a decongestant and caffeine.

Dose: Adults should take 1-2 tablets three times a day. The elderly should take one tablet three times a day. This treatment is not recommended for children under 12 years.

DOZOL

Use: A liquid short term treatment of pain associated with sleeplessness. Liquid contains paracetamol and diphenhydramine.

Dose: Adults and children over 12 should take 20ml-40ml at bedtime. Should not be taken with alcohol or concurrently with other paracetamol products. Do not take for more than seven consecutive nights without seeking medical advice. Reduce day time dose of paracetamol.

DRAMAMINE

Use: Tablets for relieving travel sickness that contain an antihistamine.

Dose: Adults should take 1-2 tablets 2-3 times a day. The first dose should be taken half an hour before starting on a journey. Children, depending on age, should be given a quarter to one tablet. This treatment is not recommended for babies under one year.

DRAPOLENE CREAM

Use: A cream which can help soothe sunburn and nappy rash, containing the antiseptics, benzalkonium chloride and cetrimide.

Dose: The cream should be applied as required.

DRISTAN DECONGESTANT TABLETS

Use: Tablets for relieving the symptoms of colds and flu. Each tablet contains aspirin, chlorpheniramine, an antihistamine, phenylephrine, a decongestant and caffeine.

Dose: Two tablets should be taken four times a day. Take a maximum of eight tablets in 24 hours. This treatment is not recommended for children under 12 years.

DRISTAN NASAL SPRAY

Use: A nasal spray for clearing nasal congestion caused by sinusitis or hayfever, containing oxymetazoline, a decongestant.

Dose: Adults should take 1-2 sprays in each nostril every 8-12 hours. This treatment is not recommended for children under six years. Do not use for longer than seven days.

DUBAM CREAM

Use: A cream for easing muscular aches and pains, containing methyl salicylate, menthol and cineole.

Dose: Apply with gentle massaging 2-3 times daily to the affected areas, avoiding broken or inflamed skin. Keep away from eyes. Wash hands after use. Do not use on children under 6 years of age.

DUBAM SPRAY

Use: A spray treatment for easing muscular aches and pains, containing rubefacients and a salicylate, an aspirin derivative.

Dose: The product should be sprayed onto the affected area for two seconds, up to four times a day. This treatment is not recommended for children under six years. Use with caution if asthmatic or allergic to aspirin.

DULCO-LAX SUPPOSITORIES

Use: A suppository for alleviating constipation, containing the stimulant laxative, bisacodyl.

Dose: One suppository should be applied in the morning. This treatment is not recommended for children under 10 years. A lower strength version is also available for children.

DULCO-LAX TABLETS

Use: Tablets for relieving constipation. They contain bisacodyl, a stimulant laxative.

Dose: 1-2 tablets should be taken on retiring. This treatment is not recommended for children under 10 years. The product is also available in liquid form and as a children's lower strength version.

DUOFILM

Use: A liquid remedy for the treatment of warts and verrucae, containing salicylic acid and lactic acid.

Dose: The liquid should be applied once or twice a day. Allow 6-12 weeks for it to take effect. Discuss with a doctor before using the product on children. This treatment is not recommended for children under six years.

DUPHALAC SOLUTION

Use: A liquid remedy for relieving constipation, containing lactulose, an osmotic laxative.

Dose: Adults should take 15 ml twice a day. Children (5-10 years) should be given 10 ml twice a day. Children (1-5 years) should be given 5 ml twice a day. Babies under one year should be given 2.5 ml – check with a pharmacist or doctor prior to use.

E45 CREAM

Use: An emollient cream for the treatment of eczema and dermatitis, which contains a mixture of oils including hypoallergenic lanolin.

Dose: The cream should be applied to the affected area 2-3 times a day as required.

EAREX EAR DROPS

Use: Ear drops for softening and removing earwax, which contain various oils including peanut oil.

Dose: Four drops of the liquid should be applied into the affected ear and a cotton wool plug applied. Repeat morning and evening for four days until the wax clears.

EAREX PLUS DROPS

Use: Ear drops for the removal of earwax, containing a mild analgesic and an ingredient for softening wax.

Dose: The ear should be filled with the liquid and plugged with cotton wool. Use twice a day for four days. This treatment is not recommended for babies under one year.

ECDYLIN SYRUP

Use: A liquid remedy for the treatment of coughs, containing diphenhydramine, an antihistamine and ammonium chloride, an expectorant.

Dose: Adults should take 5-10 ml every 2-3 hours. Children (1-12 years) should be given 2.5-5 ml according to age. Read the label for the correct dosage. This treatment is not recommended for children under one year.

ECOSTATIN

Use: This is a cream for the treatment of athlete's foot, containing econazole, an antifungal ingredient.

Dose: Apply this product twice a day to the affected part.

EFFERCITRATE SACHETS

Use: Sachets of powder containing citric acid and potassium bicarbonate, for the treatment of cystitis.

Dose: One sachet should be dissolved in water three times a day and taken after meals.

EFFERCITRATE TABLETS

Use: An effervescent tablet that helps to reduce the acidity that causes cystitis, containing citric acid and potassium citrate.

Dose: Two tablets should be dissolved in water and taken up to three times a day after meals.

EFFICO TONIC

Use: A liquid tonic for general fatigue, containing caffeine, Vitamin B1 and nicotinamide.

Dose: Adults should take 10 ml three times a day after food. Children should be given 2.5-5 ml, according to age, three times a day after food.

ELECTROLADE

Use: A powder solution for replacing the fluids and salts lost from the body during an attack of diarrhoea.

Dose: Adults should take 1-2 sachets dissolved in a measured amount of water (see instructions on the packet for correct measurements) after every loose bowel movement. Up to 16 sachets can be taken in 24 hours. Children should be given one sachet after every loose bowel movement, with up to 12 sachets in 24 hours. Consult a doctor before using this treatment on babies under two years. The product is available in a range of flavours.

ELLIMAN'S UNIVERSAL EMBROCATION

Use: An embrocation for easing muscular aches and pains, containing rubefacients.

Dose: The product should be applied to the affected area every three hours on the first day, then twice a day until the pain eases. This treatment is not recommended for children under 12 years.

ELUDRIL MOUTHWASH

Use: A mouthwash for the treatment of bad breath, sore gums and general infections of the mouth. It contains chlorhexidine, an anti-microbial.

Dose: The mouth should be rinsed with 10-15 ml of the mouthwash diluted with water, 2-3 times a day, taking care not to swallow the liquid. This treatment is not recommended for children. The product is also available as a spray.

EMULSIDERM EMOLLIENT

Use: An emollient bath additive for relieving the discomfort of eczema and dermatitis, containing various oils and an antiseptic.

Dose: The product can be added to bath water or applied directly to the skin.

ENO

Use: A powder remedy for relieving indigestion, heartburn and gastritis, containing an antacid and sodium.

Dose: One sachet or one teaspoon should be dissolved in water every 2-3 hours or as required. Take a maximum of six doses in 24 hours. This treatment is not recommended for children under 12 years. The product is also available in lemon flavour.

ENTEROSAN TABLETS

Use: Tablets to help stop diarrhoea. They contain kaolin, morphine and belladonna.

Dose: Four tablets should be taken when diarrhoea starts, followed by two tablets every three to four hours. This treatment is not recommended for children under 12 years.

ENTROTABS
Use: Tablets for the treatment of diarrhoea, containing kaolin.
Dose: Adults should take four tablets at the start of diarrhoea, then two tablets every three to four hours. Children (6-12 years) should be given one tablet every four hours. This treatment is not recommended for children under six years.

EQUILON
Use: Tablets for the treatment of irritable bowel syndrome that contain mebeverine, which helps calm intestinal spasms.
Dose: One tablet can be taken up to three times a day, preferably 20 minutes before meals. This treatment is not recommended for children under 10 years.

ESKAMEL CREAM
Use: A cream for the treatment of acne and spots, containing resorcinol and sulphur.
Dose: The cream should be applied once a day. This treatment is not recommended for children under 15 years.

ESKORNADE CAPSULES
Use: Capsules for relieving the symptoms of colds and flu. Each capsule contains phenylpropanolamine, a decongestant and diphenhydramine, an antihistamine.
Dose: One capsule should be taken every 12 hours. This treatment is not recommended for children under 12 years. The product is also available in a syrup form.

EURAX CREAM
Use: This is a cream containing crotamiton for relieving itching caused by stings, bites, hives, eczema, dermatitis and sunburn. Also for the treatment of scabies.
Dose: Adults and children over 3 years: after a warm bath, dry the skin well and rub cream into the entire body surface (excluding the face and scalp). Repeat once daily, preferably in the evening, for a total of 3-5 days. Areas where there is pus formation should be covered with a dressing impregnated with Eurax. Children under 3 years should apply as above, however do not apply more than once daily. Consult your doctor before using on infants. Patients with weeping skin conditions should not use this product, nor should those with hypersensitivity to crotamiton. Keep away from eyes and broken skin. Not recommended for pregnant women, especially in the first trimester. The product is also available as a lotion.

EURAX HC CREAM
Use: This cream contains crotamiton and the steroid, hydrocortisone,

for the treatment of eczema, dermatitis, stings, bites and hives.
Dose: The cream should be applied sparingly up to twice a day. This treatment is not recommended for children under 10 years.

EX-LAX SENNA
Use: Chocolate tablets for easing the discomfort of constipation, containing senna, a stimulant laxative.
Dose: Adults should take one tablet of chocolate when retiring. Children over six years should be given half to one tablet at bedtime. This treatment is not recommended for children under six years.

EXPULIN CHESTY COUGH LINCTUS
Use: A liquid remedy for relieving coughs, containing guaiphenesin, an expectorant.
Dose: Adults should take 10 ml every 2-3 hours. Children (3-12 years) should be given 5 ml every 2-3 hours. This treatment is not recommended for children under three years.

EXPULIN COUGH LINCTUS
Use: A liquid remedy for the treatment of coughs, containing pholcodine, a cough suppressant, chlorpheniramine, an antihistamine, and pseudoephedrine, a decongestant.
Dose: Adults should take 10 ml four times a day. Children (2-12 years) should be given 2.5-10 ml a day according to age. Read the label for the correct dosage. This treatment is not recommended for children under two years. A children's version is available.

EXPULIN DECONGESTANT FOR BABIES AND CHILDREN (LINCTUS)
Use: A sugar-free liquid remedy for relieving the symptoms of colds and flu in children. The liquid contains chlorpheniramine, an antihistamine, and ephedrine, a decongestant.
Dose: Children (3 months-12 years) should be given 2.5-15 ml, 2-3 times a day according to age. Read the label for the correct dosage. This treatment is not recommended for babies under three months.

EXPULIN DRY COUGH LINCTUS
Use: A liquid remedy for the treatment of coughs, containing pholcodine, a cough suppressant.
Dose: 5 ml should be taken three to four times a day. This treatment is not recommended for children under 12 years.

EXTEROL EAR DROPS
Use: Ear drops for removing earwax, containing softening ingredients.
Dose: 5 drops should be applied into the affected ear once or twice a day, for 3-4 days.

EYE DEW

Use: An eye drop containing distilled witch hazel, naphazoline hydrochloride and benzalkonium chloride, for clearer whites of the eye and sparkling eyes.

Dose: One or two drops in both eyes. Do not use with soft contact lenses. If you suffer from any eye disease (e.g glaucoma) or high blood pressure, heart disease, diabetes, hyperthyroidism or depression, consult a doctor before use.

FAMEL EXPECTORANT

Use: A liquid remedy for coughs, containing guaiphenesin, an expectorant.

Dose: Adults should take 20 ml every 2-4 hours if required. Children (1-12 years) should be given 5-10 ml, according to age. Read the label for the correct dosage. This treatment is not recommended for children under one year.

FAMEL ORIGINAL

Use: A liquid remedy for the treatment of coughs, containing codeine, a cough suppressant and creosote.

Dose: 10-15 ml should be taken three times a day. This treatment is not recommended for children under 12 years.

FEDRIL EXPECTORANT

Use: A liquid remedy for the treatment of coughs, containing diphenhydramine, an antihistamine, ammonium chloride, an expectorant and menthol.

Dose: Adults should take 5-10 ml 3-4 times a day. Children (2-12 years) should be given 2.5-5 ml, according to age. Read the label for the correct dosage. This treatment is not recommended for children under two years.

FEDRIL TICKLY COUGH

Use: A liquid remedy for the treatment of coughs, containing cetylp yearidium, an antiseptic, ipecacuanha and ammonium chloride, which are both expectorants, lemon oil, purified honey, glycerin and citric acid.

Dose: Adults should take 15 ml every 2-3 hours. Children (2-12 years) should be given 5-10 ml, according to age. Read the label for the correct dosage. This treatment is not recommended for children under two years.

FELDENE P GEL

Use: This is a gel for the treatment of muscular aches and pains, containing piroxicam, a non-steroidal anti-inflammatory (NSAID).

Dose: The product should be applied to the affected area up to four times a day. This treatment is not recommended for children under 12 years.

FEMERON
Use: A cream for the treatment of thrush, containing 2 per cent miconazole nitrate.
Dose: The product should be applied to the external vaginal area morning and evening.

FEMERON SOFT PESSARY
Use: A pessary for the treatment of thrush, containing 1200 mg of miconazole nitrate.
Dose: One pessary should be inserted into the vagina at night. This is a single-dose treatment.

FEMINAX
Use: A tablet remedy for relieving period pain, containing paracetamol, codeine, caffeine and an antispasmodic.
Dose: 1-2 tablets should be taken every four hours when necessary. Take a maximum of six tablets in 24 hours.

FENBID GEL
Use: A gel containing ibuprofen, a non-steroidal anti-inflammatory (NSAID), for the treatment of muscular aches and pains.
Dose: The gel should be massaged into the affected area up to four times a day. This treatment is not recommended for children under 14 years. The product is also available as a cream.

FENNINGS CALAMINE LOTION
Use: A lotion for the relief of sunburn and general sore unbroken skin conditions, containing calamine and zinc oxide.
Dose: Dab the lotion on the affected parts with cotton wool and allow to dry. For external use only.

FENNINGS CALAMINE CREAM
Use: A cream for the relief of mild sunburn and dry and chapped hands, contains calamine.
Dose: Apply to the affected parts and rub in gently. For external use only.

FENNINGS CHILDREN'S COOLING POWDERS
Use: An analgesic powder which can be used for general pain relief, containing 50 mg of paracetamol in 1 ml.
Dose: Take a maximum of four doses in 24 hours. The powder should be dissolved in water. Babies (3 months-1 year) should be given one powder. Children (1-6 years) should be given two powders. Children

(6-12 years) should be given four powders. This treatment is not recommended for babies under three months.

FENNINGS LITTLE HEALERS

Use: A tablet for the treatment of coughs, containing ipecacuanha, an expectorant.

Dose: Adults should take two tablets three times a day. Children (5-12 years) should take one tablet. This treatment is not recommended for children under five years.

FENOX NASAL DROPS

Use: Nasal drops for relieving nasal congestion caused by sinusitis or hayfever, containing phenylephrine, a decongestant.

Dose: Adults should take 4-5 drops into each nostril morning and night and every four hours if required. Children (5-12 years) should take two drops in each nostril night and morning, and every four hours if required. This treatment is not recommended for children under five years. Do not use longer than seven days. The product is also available as a spray.

FIERY JACK

Use: A cream rub for alleviating muscular aches and pains, containing rubefacients.

Dose: The product should be applied to the affected area twice a day. This treatment is not recommended for children under six years.

FLUOR-A-DAY TABLETS

Use: Tablets containing flouride.

Dose: 1.1 mg for children up to four years of age; 2.2 mg for children over four years. Check if the local water supply contains flouride before using and adjust dose accordingly.

FRADOR

Use: A liquid treatment for mouth ulcers, containing antiseptic and astringent ingredients.

Dose: The liquid should be applied to the ulcer with the applicator provided, four times a day after meals and before retiring to bed. This treatment is not recommended for children.

FULL MARKS LIQUID

Use: A liquid treatment for head lice and other infestations, containing phenothrin.

Dose: The liquid should be rubbed into the scalp and the hair combed whilst wet, then allowed to dry naturally. The treatment should be left in for at least 12 hours, then washed out. This treatment is not recommended for babies under six months.

FULL MARKS LOTION
Use: A lotion for the treatment of head lice, containing phenothrin and alcohol.
Dose: The lotion should be rubbed into dry hair and left in for two hours or overnight. Wash and comb through hair while it is wet. This treatment is not recommended for babies under six months.

FULL MARKS MOUSSE
Use: A mousse for the treatment of head lice, containing phenothrin.
Dose: Shake well turning it downward to dispense mousse. Apply sufficient mousse to dry hair until all the hair and scalp are thoroughly moistened. Allow to dry naturally – do not use artificial heat – and leave for 30 minutes. Then shampoo and rinse as normal. Comb with a fine-toothed comb while still wet to remove the dead lice and eggs. Children under 6 months should be treated under medical supervision. Do not use more than once a week and for not more than three consecutive weeks.

FUNGEDERM CREAM
Use: Cream for the treatment of fungal skin infections. Cream contains clotrimazole.
Dose: Apply twice daily. To prevent relapse, treatment should continue for 10 days after all signs of infection have disappeared.

FYBOGEL
Use: These are granules for the treatment of constipation and irritable bowel syndrome, containing ispaghula husk, which is a bulking agent.
Dose: Adults should dissolve one sachet of the granules in water and drink after a meal, twice a day. Children (6-12 years) should be given 2.5-5 ml of granules twice a day. The product should be taken with plenty of liquid, and not before bedtime. This treatment is not recommended for children under six years. The product is available in various flavours.

FYNNON CALCIUM ASPIRIN
Use: A soluble analgesic which can be used for general pain relief, containing 500 mg of aspirin.
Dose: 1-2 tablets should be dissolved in water and taken every four hours if required. Take a maximum of eight tablets in 24 hours. This treatment is not recommended for children under 12 years.

FYNNON SALTS
Use: A powder remedy for relieving the symptoms of constipation. The powder contains sodium sulphate, an osmotic laxative.
Dose: 5 ml should be taken once or twice a day dissolved in water. This treatment is not recommended for children under 12 years.

GALENPHOL ADULT LINCTUS

Use: A liquid remedy for the treatment of coughs, containing pholcodine, a cough suppressant.
Dose: Adults should take 10-15 ml 3-4 times a day. Children (5-12 years) should be given one dose. This treatment is not recommended for children under five years.

GALENPHOL PAEDIATRIC

Use: A liquid remedy for the treatment of coughs, containing pholcodine, a cough suppressant.
Dose: Children (1-5 years) should be given 5-10 ml three times a day. Babies (3-12 months) should be given 2.5 ml. This treatment is not recommended for babies under three months.

GALLOWAY'S COUGH SYRUP

Use: A liquid remedy for coughs, containing ipecacuanha and squill, both expectorants.
Dose: Adults should take 10 ml three to four times a day. Children under 10 years should be given half the adult dose. Read the label for the correct dosage.

GALPAMOL

Use: Analgesic 5 ml sachets containing paracetamol suspension.
Dose: Not to be given more frequently than every 4 hours and not more than 4 doses in 24 hours. Babies 3 months-1 year should take only half to one sachet. Children 1-6 years should take one to two sachets.

GALPHARM FLU RELIEF CAPSULES

Use: Capsules for the symptomatic relief of colds and flu. Capsules contain paracetamol and phenylephrine hydrochloride.
Dose: Adults and children over 12 should take one capsule every four hours to a maximum of four capsules in 24 hours. Do not give to children under 12 years except on medical advice. Do not take if pregnant or breastfeeding and do not take with any other paracetamol-containing products.

GALPROFEN

Use: Analgesic tablets containing ibuprofen.
Dose: Adults and children over 12 should take one or two tablets up to three times a day with or after food. Maximum 6 tablets in 24 hours. Do not take if you have an ulcer or other stomach disorder.

GALPROFEN LONG LASTING CAPSULES

Use: Analgesic capsules containing ibuprofen for up to 12 hour pain relief.

Dose: Adults and children over 12 should take two capsules to be taken each morning and evening. Not recommended for children under 12 years except on medical advice.

GALPSEUD
Use: Tablets for the treatment of sinusitis, containing pseudoephedrine, a decongestant.
Dose: Adults should take one tablet four times a day. This treatment is not recommended for children under 12 years. The product is also available as a liquid.

GASTROCOTE LIQUID
Use: A liquid remedy for the treatment of upset stomachs, indigestion and heartburn, containing sodium, an antacid, and an alginate.
Dose: 5-15 ml should be taken four times a day after meals and on retiring. This treatment is not recommended for children under six years. The product is also available in tablet form.

GAVISCON 250
Use: A tablet remedy for indigestion and heartburn, containing an antacid, sodium, and an alginate.
Dose: Two tablets should be chewed as needed. This treatment is not recommended for children under 12 years. The product is also available in extra strength form, Gaviscon 500, and in a liquid version, Gaviscon Advance.

GELCOSAL
Use: A gel for the treatment of psoriasis and chronic scaling dermatitis. Gel contains strong coal tar solution, pine tar and salicylic acid.
Dose: Apply to the skin twice daily. Avoid contact with eyes or mucous membranes.

GELCOTAR LIQUID
Use: A liquid for the treatment of dandruff, containing coal tar.
Dose: The liquid should be used as a shampoo twice a week.

GELTEARS
Use: Opthalmic gel for the relief of dry eyes. Contains carbomer 940.
Dose: One drop three or four times daily as required. May cause transient blurring on instillation. Should not be used when wearing soft contact lenses.

GERMOLENE ANTISEPTIC WIPES
Use: Cleansing wipes for the treatment of minor wounds and skin irritations, impregnated with an antiseptic. The wipes contain benzalkonium chloride and chlorohexidine gluconate.
Dose: Use to clean wounds as required.

GERMOLENE CREAM

Use: An antiseptic cream for the treatment of minor wounds and irritations of the skin, containing phenol and chlorohexidine gluconate.
Dose: The cream should be applied to the affected area, and covered with a dressing if necessary.

GERMOLENE NEW SKIN

Use: A liquid that forms a water- and germ-proof barrier to protect minor wounds.
Dose: The liquid should be applied to the cut or graze and allowed to dry.

GERMOLENE OINTMENT

Use: An antiseptic ointment for the treatment of minor wounds and irritations of the skin. It contains zinc oxide, methyl salicylate, phenol lanolin and octaphonium chloride.
Dose: The product should be applied to the affected area or smeared onto a dressing.

GERMOLOIDS CREAM

Use: A cream treatment for piles, containing lidocaine, a mild local anaesthetic, and zinc oxide, an astringent.
Dose: The product should be applied to the affected area twice a day and after each bowel movement, with no more than four applications in one day. This treatment is not recommended for children under 12 years. The product is also available as suppositories and as an ointment.

GLUTAROL

Use: A liquid treatment for warts and verrucae, containing glutaraldehyde.
Dose: The product should be applied to the wart or verruca twice a day.

GODDARD'S EMBROCATION

Use: An embrocation for relieving muscular aches and pains, containing a rubefacient.
Dose: The product should be applied to the affected area once or twice a day or as required. This treatment is not recommended for children under six years.

GOLDEN EYE OINTMENT

Use: Eye ointment for treating infections of the eye including conjunctivitis and styes. It contains dibromopropamidine, an anti-microbial.
Dose: The product should be applied to the affected eye once or twice a day.

GYNO-PEVARYL CREAM
Use: White non-staining cream for the treatment of vulvitis associated with candidal vaginitis. Contains econazole nitrate.
Dose: Apply cream to the vulva and perianal region and/or genitalia of the partner daily for 14 days.

HACTOS COUGH MIXTURE
Use: A liquid treatment for the symptomatic relief of coughs, colds and catarrh. Brown liquid contains capiscum tincture, peppermint oil, anise oil and clove oil.
Dose: Adults should take two 5 ml spoonsful morning, afternoon and evening. Children 7-12 years should take 5 ml in the morning, afternoon and evening. This medicine may cause drowsiness.

HALLS SOOTHERS
Use: Medicated sweets for easing sore throats, containing menthol and eucalyptus.
Dose: The sweets should be dissolved in the mouth as required.

HANSAPLAST THERMO HERBAL HEAT PLASTER
Use: For the symptomatic relief of muscular and rheumatic pain in conditions such as stiff neck, painful shoulder, myalgia, lumbago, backache, shooting pains, rheumatism, sciatica and neuralgia. Plaster contains capisci fructus acer (cayenne), capsicum extract and arnica extract.
Dose: Adults and children over 12 should apply to clean, dry unbroken skin. The painful area should be fully covered and the plaster left in place as long as the sensation of warmth continues, but not more than two days. Not recommended for children under 12 years. Wash hands after handling plaster. Avoid use in pregnancy and lactation. Do not apply to open wounds, bruises or on broken skin.

HAPPINOSE
Use: Ointment for the symptomatic relief of nasal congestion associated with the common cold, catarrh, head colds and hayfever. Contains menthol with natural essential oils.
Dose: Blow the nose before application. Apply up to 1 cm of ointment in and around each nostril using the little finger and inhale. Re-apply every four hours as required. Children 10 years and over as for adults but use 0.5 cm, children 5-9 years use 0.25 cm. Do not use on children under 5 years.

HAY-CROM HAY FEVER EYE DROPS
Use: Eye drops for easing the symptoms of hayfever, containing sodium cromoglycate, an anti-inflammatory.
Dose: 1-2 drops should be applied into each affected eye up to four

times a day. This treatment is not recommended for children under five years.

HAYMINE

Use: Tablets for relieving the symptoms of hayfever, containing chlorpheniramine, an antihistamine, and ephedrine, a decongestant.

Dose: One tablet should be taken in the morning, and another tablet can be taken at night if necessary. This treatment is not recommended for children under 12 years.

HC45 HYDROCORTISONE CREAM

Use: A hydrocortisone cream for the treatment of eczema, dermatitis, stings, bites and hives.

Dose: The product should be applied to the affected area sparingly once or twice a day. This treatment is not recommended for children under 10 years.

HEALTHY FEET

Use: A treatment for athlete's foot, containing undecylenic acid, an antifungal ingredient.

Dose: The product should be applied to the affected area as often as is necessary.

HEDEX

Use: Analgesic tablets that can be used for general pain relief, containing 500 mg of paracetamol.

Dose: Adults should take two tablets up to four times a day. Take a maximum of eight tablets in 24 hours. Children (6-12 years) should be given half of one tablet every four hours, with a maximum of four tablets in 24 hours. This treatment is not recommended for children under six years.

HEDEX EXTRA

Use: Analgesic tablets which can be used for general pain relief, containing 500 mg of paracetamol and caffeine.

Dose: Two tablets should be taken up to four times a day. Take a maximum of eight tablets in 24 hours. This treatment is not suitable for children under 12 years.

HEDEX IBUPROFEN

Use: Analgesic tablets for general pain relief, containing 200 mg of ibuprofen.

Dose: 1-2 tablets should be taken up to three times a day. Take a maximum of six tablets in 24 hours. This treatment is not recommended for children under 12 years.

HEMOCANE CREAM
Use: A cream treatment for the treatment of piles, containing lignocaine, a mild local anaesthetic and zinc oxide, an astringent.
Dose: The cream should be applied morning and night, and after each bowel movement. This treatment is not recommended for children under 12 years.

HERPETAD COLD SORE CREAM
Use: A cream for the treatment of cold sores, containing aciclovir, an antiviral.
Dose: The cream should be applied as soon as a cold sore tingling is felt, and applied to the sore every four hours, five times a day for five days.

HEWLETTS CREAM
Use: A white scented cream for the treatment of nappy rash, nursing hygiene and chapped and sore hands. Contains zinc oxide, hydrous wool fat, oleic acid, arachis oil, oil of rose and white soft paraffin.
Dose: Apply evenly at every nappy change. Do not apply to large areas of broken skin. For external use only.

HILL'S BALSAM CHESTY COUGH LIQUID
Use: A liquid remedy for the treatment of coughs, containing guaiphenesin, an expectorant.
Dose: 5-10 ml should be taken every two to four hours. Take a maximum of 60 ml in 24 hours. This treatment is not recommended for children under 12 years.

HILL'S BALSAM CHESTY COUGH LIQUID FOR CHILDREN
Use: A liquid sugar-free remedy for relieving coughs, containing ipecacuanha, citric acid and capsicum, all expectorants, and benzoin, saccharin and orange oil.
Dose: 2.5-5 ml should be given three times a day and at bedtime, according to age. Read the label for the correct dosage.

HILL'S BALSAM DRY COUGH LIQUID
Use: A liquid remedy for the treatment of coughs, containing pholcodine, a cough suppressant.
Dose: 5 ml should be taken 3-4 times a day. This treatment is not recommended for children under 12 years.

HILL'S BALSAM EXTRA STRONG 2-IN-1 PASTILLES
Use: Herbal pastilles for soothing the symptoms of colds and flu, containing ipecacuanha, menthol and peppermint.
Dose: One pastille should be dissolved in the mouth as required, with

a maximum of 10 pastilles in 24 hours. Children over 12 years should be given a maximum of seven pastilles in 24 hours. This treatment is not recommended for children under 12 years.

HIOXYL CREAM

Use: White non-greasy cream for the treatment of minor wounds, leg ulcers and pressure sores. Contains stabilised hydrogen peroxide.
Dose: Apply freely using a piece of lint or gauze. Cover with a dressing if necessary. Repeat as required.

HIRUDOID CREAM

Use: A cream to aid the healing of minor bruises, containing heparinoid, an ingredient that helps resolve bruising.
Dose: The product should be applied to the bruise four times a day. This treatment is not recommended for children under four years. The product is also available as a gel.

HYDROMOL CREAM

Use: An emollient cream for relieving the discomfort of eczema and dermatitis, containing a mixture of oils including peanut oil.
Dose: The cream should be applied liberally and used as often as required.

HYDROMOL EMOLLIENT

Use: An emollient bath additive for relieving the discomfort of eczema and dermatitis, containing a mixture of oils.
Dose: 1-3 capfuls of the liquid should be added to a shallow bath.

IBUFEM

Use: Analgesic tablets for the relief of period pain. Tablets contain ibuprofen.
Dose: Adults and children over 12 years should take two capsules every four hours up to a maximum of six tablets in 24 hours. Not recommended for children under 12 years except on medical advice.

IBULEVE GEL

Use: A gel for the treatment of muscular aches and pains, containing ibuprofen, a non-steroidal anti-inflammatory (NSAID).
Dose: The gel should be massaged into the affected area up to three times a day. This treatment is not recommended for children under 12 years. The product is also available in a spray and as a mousse.

IBULEVE SPORTS

Use: A gel for the treatment of muscular aches and pains, containing ibuprofen, a non-steroidal anti-inflammatory (NSAID).
Dose: The product should be massaged into the affected area up to

three times a day. This treatment is not recommended for children under 12 years.

IBUSPRAY

Use: A spray for relieving muscular aches and pains, containing ibuprofen, a non-steroidal anti-inflammatory (NSAID).

Dose: The product should be sprayed onto the affected part and massaged in 3-4 times a day. This treatment is not recommended for children under 12 years.

IMODIUM CAPSULES

Use: Capsules to help stop diarrhoea, containing loperamide.

Dose: Two capsules should be taken at the start of an attack of diarrhoea, and then one capsule after every loose bowel movement. Take a maximum of eight capsules in 24 hours. This treatment is not recommended for children under 12 years. The product is also available in liquid form.

IMUDERM THERAPEUTIC OIL

Use: An emollient bath additive for the treatment of eczema and dermatitis, containing various oils.

Dose: 15-30 ml of the oil can be added to the bath water or applied directly to the skin.

INADINE

Use: A non-stick dressing to be applied to minor burns and scalds, containing povidone iodine – an anti-microbial.

Dose: The product should be applied as required.

INFACOL

Use: A liquid remedy for relieving wind and colic in babies, containing simethicone, an anti-wind ingredient. A measure is supplied.

Dose: One measured dose of 0.5 ml should be given before each feed. The liquid can be used from birth onwards.

INFADERM THERAPEUTIC OIL

Use: A clear solution for the treatment of dry skin conditions including eczema, contact dermatitis, ichthyosis, psoriasis, serile pruritis, containing almond oil and liquid paraffin light.

Dose: Adults and children should add 15ml-30ml to a bath. Infants (using small bath) use up to 15ml. Can be used as an after bath emollient.

INFADROPS

Use: An analgesic liquid for general pain relief, containing 100 mg of paracetamol. A measuring pipette is supplied.

Dose: A maximum of four doses can be given in 24 hours. Babies (3-12 months) should be given 0.8 ml. Babies (1-2 years) should be given 1.2 ml. Children (2-3 years) should be given 1.6 ml. This treatment is not recommended for babies under three months unless advised otherwise by a doctor.

INTRALGIN
Use: A gel for the treatment of muscular aches and pains, containing a rubefacient and a local anaesthetic.
Dose: The gel should be massaged gently into the affected area as required.

IONAX
Use: A facial scrub for treating spots and acne, containing abrasive and antibacterial ingredients.
Dose: The face should be moistened and the gel rubbed in for 1-2 minutes, then rinsed off. The treatment should be used once or twice a day. This treatment is not recommended for children under 12 years.

IONIL T
Use: A medicated shampoo for the treatment of dandruff, containing coal tar and an antiseptic.
Dose: Should be used as a shampoo once or twice a week.

ISOGEL
Use: A granule remedy for relieving the symptoms of constipation, diarrhoea and irritable bowel syndrome. The granules contain ispaghula husk, a bulking laxative.
Dose: Adults should take 10 ml dissolved in water once or twice a day. Children (6-12 years) should be given 5 ml once or twice a day. The granules should be taken with plenty of fluid and it is advisable not to take the treatment at bedtime. This treatment is not recommended for children under six years.

ISOPTO FRIN
Use: A solution for the temporary relief of redness of the eye due to minor irritations. Solution contains phenylephrine hydrochloride in an aqueous vehicle containing hypromellose.
Dose: Take one or two drops into the eye up to four times a day. If you have any eye disease or have had eye surgery or if you are being treated for high blood pressure or depression, consult your doctor before using these drops. Continued use may increase redness. Not to be used by contact lens wearers.

JACKSON'S ALL FOURS
Use: A liquid remedy for the treatment of coughs, containing

guaiphesin, a cough suppressant.

Dose: 10-20 ml should be taken at bedtime or every four hours if necessary. This treatment is not recommended for children under 12 years.

JACKSON'S FEBRIFUGE

Use: This is a liquid remedy for relieving the symptoms of colds and flu, containing sodium salicylate, an ingredient related to aspirin.

Dose: Adults should take 5-10 ml in water every six hours or three times a day. The elderly should take half the adult dose. This treatment is not recommended for children under 12 years.

J COLLIS BROWNE'S MIXTURE

Use: This is a liquid remedy for the treatment of diarrhoea and digestive upsets, containing morphine.

Dose: Adults should take 10-15 ml every four hours. Children (6-12 years) should be given 5 ml every four hours. This treatment is not recommended for children under six years. The product is also available in tablet form.

JELONET

Use: A sterile gauze dressing for the treatment of burns and scalds. It is impregnated with soft paraffin which prevents fibres from sticking to the burn.

Dose: The product should be applied to the affected area as required.

JOY-RIDES

Use: Tablets for the prevention of travel sickness, containing hyoscine, an anti-spasmodic.

Dose: Adults should take two tablets 20 minutes before the start of a journey or at the onset of nausea. The dose may be repeated after six hours if necessary. Children over three years should be given half to two tablets depending on age, with a maximum of two doses in 24 hours. Check instructions on the label for the correct dosage. This treatment is not recommended for children under three years.

JUNGLE FORMULA BITE AND STING RELIEF CREAM

Use: This is a cream for the treatment of bites and stings. It contains a steroid.

Dose: The product should be applied sparingly to the affected area once or twice a day. Do not use for more than seven days. This treatment is not recommended for children under 10 years.

JUNIOR DISPROL PARACETAMOL TABLETS

Use: A lime flavoured, soluble analgesic tablet for general pain relief. Each tablet contains 120 mg of paracetemol.

Dose: A maximum of four doses may be taken in 24 hours. For children (1-6 years) dissolve 1-2 tablets in water every four hours if required. Children (6-12 years) should be given 2-4 tablets every four hours. This treatment is not recommended for babies under one year.

JUNIOR KAO-C
Use: A liquid remedy for stopping diarrhoea in children, containing kaolin.
Dose: Children should be given 5-20 ml according to age, three times a day. Check the label for the correct dosage. This treatment is not recommended for babies under one year.

JUNIOR MELTUS EXPECTORANT
Use: A liquid remedy for the treatment of coughs, containing guaiphesin, an expectorant, cetylp yearidium, an antiseptic, purified honey and sucrose.
Dose: Children over six years should be given 10 ml 3-4 times a day. Children (1-6 years) should be given 5 ml 3-4 times a day. This treatment is not suitable for children under one year. Sugar- and colour-free versions are also available.

JUNO JUNIPAH SALTS
Use: A powder remedy for relieving the discomfort of constipation. The powders contain sodium sulphate, an osmotic laxative.
Dose: 20 ml should be given once or twice a day. This treatment is not suitable for children under 12 years. The product is also available in tablet form.

KAMILLOSAN
Use: This is an ointment for the treatment of nappy rash, containing lanolin and camomile extract.
Dose: The cream should be applied to clean dry skin at each nappy change.

KARVOL DECONGESTANT TABLETS
Use: Capsules for relieving the symptoms of colds and flu, containing various decongestant oils.
Dose: For babies over three months, children, adults and the elderly, the capsules contents should be squeezed onto a pillow or onto sheets and should be inhaled while sleeping. Adults can also squeeze a capsule into a bowl of hot water and inhale. For young children a capsule can be squeezed onto a handkerchief or clothing.

KLN
Use: A liquid remedy for stopping diarrhoea in children, containing kaolin.

Dose: Children should be given 5-10 ml, according to age, after every loose bowel movement for up to 24 hours. Check the label for the correct dosage. This treatment is not recommended for babies under six months.

KOLANTICON

Use: A liquid gel solution for relieving gastritis, indigestion and heartburn, containing antacid and an antispasmodic.
Dose: 10-20 ml should be taken every four hours. This treatment is not recommended for children under 12 years.

KWELLS

Use: Tablets for preventing travel sickness, containing hyoscine, an anti-spasmodic.
Dose: Adults should take one tablet every six hours. Take a maximum of three tablets in 24 hours. Children over 10 years should be given half the adult dose. This treatment is not recommended for children under 10 years. The product is also available as a children's version.

KY JELLY

Use: A lubricating gel for alleviating vaginal dryness.
Dose: A little of the gel should be applied to the vagina as required. The product is also available as pessaries.

LABITON

Use: A liquid remedy for alleviating general fatigue, containing alcohol, caffeine, vitamin B1 and dried extract of kola nut.
Dose: 10-20 ml should be taken twice a day. This treatment is not recommended for children under 12 years.

LABOSEPT PASTILLES

Use: Pastilles for relieving sore throats, containing dequalinium, an antibacterial.
Dose: One pastille should be sucked every 3-4 hours. Take a maximum of eight pastilles in 24 hours. This treatment is not recommended for children under 10 years.

LACITOL

Use: A powder remedy for the treatment of constipation, containing lactitol, an osmotic laxative.
Dose: Adults should take 1-2 sachets twice a day, either mixed in a cold drink or sprinkled over food. A maximum of four sachets should be taken in a day. Children (6-12 years) should be given half to one sachet a day. Children (1-6 years) should be given one quarter to half a sachet per day. This treatment is not recommended for babies under the age of one year.

LACTO-CALAMINE LOTION
Use: A lotion for soothing sunburn, containing calamine and zinc oxide.
Dose: The lotion should be applied as required

LANACANE CREME
Use: A cream for relieving bites, stings and sunburn, containing a local anaesthetic.
Dose: The product should be applied to the affected area three times a day.

LANACORT CREME
Use: A cream for the treatment of eczema and dermatitis, containing hydrocortisone, a steroid.
Dose: The cream should be applied sparingly once or twice a day. This treatment is not recommended for children under 10 years. The product is also available as an ointment.

LASONIL
Use: An ointment for the treatment of bruises containing heparinoid, an ingredient that helps to resolve bruising.
Dose: The product should be applied two to three times a day to the affected area.

LAXOBERAL
Use: A liquid remedy for constipation, containing sodium picosulphate, a stimulant laxative.
Dose: 2.5-15 ml should be given at night, depending on age. This treatment is not recommended for children under two years.

LEMSIP BREATHE EASY
Use: Sachets of powder for relieving the symptoms of colds and flu, containing paracetamol, phenylephrine, a decongestant, and vitamin C.
Dose: One sachet should be dissolved in hot water every four hours or as required. Take a maximum of four sachets in 24 hours. This treatment is not recommended for children under 12 years.

LEMSIP CHESTY COUGH
Use: A liquid remedy for the treatment of coughs, containing guaiphenesin.
Dose: Adults should take 10-20 ml three to four times a day. Children (2-12 years) should be given 5-10 ml, according to age. Read the label for the correct dosage. This treatment is not recommended for children under two years.

LEMSIP COMBINED RELIEF CAPSULES
Use: Capsules for relieving the symptoms of colds and flu, containing paracetamol, phenylephrine, a decongestant, and caffeine.
Dose: Two capsules should be taken every 3-4 hours. Take a maximum of eight capsules in 24 hours. This treatment is not recommended for children under 12 years.

LEMSIP DRY COUGH
Use: A liquid remedy for relieving coughs, containing honey, lemon oil, glycerol and citric acid.
Dose: Adults should take 10 ml 3-4 times a day. Children under 12 years should be given 5 ml 3-4 times a day. Read the label for the correct dosage.

LEMSIP MAXIMUM STRENGTH
Use: A lemon flavoured powder in sachets, for relieving the symptoms of colds and flu. Each sachet contains paracetamol, phenylephrine, a decongestant, and vitamin C.
Dose: One sachet should be dissolved in hot water every 4-6 hours or as required. Take a maximum of four sachets in 24 hours. This treatment is not recommended for children under 12 years.

LEMSIP ORIGINAL
Use: A lemon flavoured powder for relieving the symptoms of colds and flu, containing paracetamol, phenylephrine, a decongestant and vitamin C.
Dose: One sachet should be dissolved in hot water every four hours or as required. Take a maximum of four sachets in 24 hours. This treatment is not recommended for children under 12 years.

LEMSIP PHARMACY POWDER + PARACETAMOL
Use: A lemon flavoured powder in sachets for relieving the symptoms of colds and flu. Each sachet contains paracetamol, pseudoephedrine, a decongestant, and vitamin C.
Dose: One sachet should be dissolved in hot water every four hours if required. Take a maximum of four sachets in 24 hours. This treatment is not recommended for children under 12 years.

LEMSIP PHARMACY POWER CAPS
Use: Capsules for relieving the symptoms of colds and flu, containing ibuprofen and pseudoephedrine, a decongestant.
Dose: Two capsules should be taken every four hours. Take a maximum of four capsules in 24 hours. This treatment is not recommended for children under 12 years.

LENIUM

Use: A medicated shampoo for the treatment of dandruff, containing selenium sulphide.

Dose: Should be used as a shampoo twice a week until the dandruff clears, then used as required. This treatment is not recommended for children under five years.

LEVONELE

Use: Emergency contraception within 72 hours of unprotected sexual intercourse or failure of a contraceptive method. Tablets contain levonorgestrel.

Dose: Adult women 16 years or over should take one tablet as soon as possible (and no later than 72 hours) after unprotected intercourse. Take the second tablet 12 hours (and no later than 16 hours) after the first tablet. If the patient vomits within three hours of taking either tablet, another tablet should be taken immediately and the doctor, family planning clinic or pharmacist contacted for advice and more tablets. Not recommended for use by girls under the age of 16 years without medical supervision. Should not be used if the woman is pregnant.

LIBROFEM

Use: Pink analgesic tablets for the treatment of period pain, headache, migraine, muscular pain, backache and feverishness. Contains ibuprofen.

Dose: Adults and children over 12 years should take an initial dose of two tablets with a glass of water, then one or two every 4 hours. No more than six tablets in 24 hours. Patients with stomach ulcers or other stomach disorders should not use this product. Caution in patients who are asthmatic, sensitive to aspirin, pregnant or receiving medical treatment.

LIQUFRUTA GARLIC

Use: A liquid remedy for the treatment of coughs, containing guaiphenesin, an expectorant.

Dose: Adults should take 10-15 ml three times a day and at bedtime. Children (3-12 years) should be given 10 ml. Children (1-3 years) should be given 5 ml. This treatment is not recommended for children under one year.

LLOYDS CREAM

Use: A cream rub for the treatment of muscular aches and pains. It contains a rubefacient and a salicylate, an aspirin derivative.

Dose: The cream should be applied to the affected area up to three times a day. This treatment is not recommended for children under six years.

LYCLEAR CREME RINSE

Use: A lotion treatment containing permethrin for head lice and other similar infestations.

Dose: The lotion should be massaged into the hair and scalp after shampooing, then left for 10 minutes and washed out. The hair should be combed through while still wet. This treatment is not recommended for babies under six months.

LYPSYL COLD SORE GEL

Use: A gel for the treatment of cold sores. It contains lignocaine, a local anaesthetic, cetrimide, an antiseptic, and zinc sulphate, an astringent.

Dose: The cream should be applied to the cold sore 3-4 times a day.

MAALOX PLUS SUSPENSION

Use: A liquid remedy for relieving indigestion, heartburn and trapped wind. It contains an antacid and simethicone, an antiflatulent.

Dose: 5-10 ml should be taken four times a day after meals, and at bedtime. This treatment is not recommended for children under 12 years. The product is also available in tablet form.

MAALOX SUSPENSION

Use: A liquid for relieving indigestion and heartburn, containing antacids.

Dose: 10-20 ml should be taken four times a day 20-60 minutes after meals, and on retiring for the night. This treatment is not recommended for children under 12 years.

MACKENZIES SMELLING SALTS

Use: Liquid smelling salts for easing nasal congestion, containing ammonia with eucalyptus oil.

Dose: The vapour should be inhaled as required. This treatment is not recommended for babies under three months.

MACLEAN

Use: Antacid tablets for relieving indigestion and heartburn.

Dose: 1-2 tablets should be sucked or chewed as required. Take a maximum of 16 tablets in 24 hours. This treatment is not recommended for children under 12 years.

MAGNESIUM SULPHATE PASTE BP

Use: This is a non-brand name paste for 'drawing out' boils. It contains magnesium sulphate, phenol and glycerol.

Dose: The paste should be stirred and then applied to the boil. The area should then be covered with a clean, dry dressing.

MANDANOL
Use: An analgesic tablet for general pain relief and feverish conditions, containing 500 mg of paracetamol.
Dose: 2 tablets should be taken every four hours, not more frequently than four hours. Take a maximum of eight tablets in 24 hours. Children (6-12 years) should take half to one tablet every four hours as required, not more than four hourly. Maximum of four tablets in 24 hours. Not to be given to children under 6 years. Use with caution in cases of severe liver or kidney problems.

MANEVAC
Use: A granular remedy for relieving constipation, containing fibre and senna, a stimulant laxative.
Dose: The granules should be placed on the tongue and swallowed with plenty of water, without chewing. Adults should take 5-10 ml once or twice a day. Children (5-12 years) should be given 5 ml once a day. Pregnant women should take 5-10 ml every morning and evening. This treatment is not recommended for children under five years.

MASNODERM
Use: A cream treatment for athlete's foot, containing the antifungal ingredient, clotrimazole.
Dose: The cream should be applied to the affected area twice a day for four weeks.

MAXIMUM STRENGTH ASPRO CLEAR
Use: An effervescent analgesic tablet for general pain relief, containing 500 mg of aspirin.
Dose: 1-2 tablets should be dissolved in water every four hours. Take a maximum of eight tablets in 24 hours. This treatment is not recommended for children under 12 years.

MEDIJEL
Use: A gel for the treatment of sore gums, bad breath and mouth ulcers, containing lidocaine, a local anaesthetic.
Dose: The gel should be applied every 20 minutes or as necessary.

MEDINOL OVER 6 PARACETAMOL ORAL SUSPENSION
Use: A strawberry flavoured analgesic liquid for general pain relief, which is sugar- and colour-free. It contains 250 mg of paracetamol in every 5 ml.
Dose: Take a maximum of four doses in 24 hours. Children (6-12 years) should be given 5-10 ml every four hours if required. For children under six years, use Medinol Under 6.

MEDINOL UNDER 6 PARACETAMOL ORAL SUSPENSION

Use: A strawberry flavoured analgesic liquid for general pain relief, which is sugar- and colour-free. It contains 120 mg of paracetamol in every 5 ml.

Dose: Take a maximum of four doses in 24 hours. Babies (3-12 months) should be given 2.5-5 ml every four hours if required. Children (1-5 years) should be given 10 ml every four hours. Children over five years should be given 15-20 ml. This treatment is not recommended for babies under three months unless advised otherwise by a doctor.

MEDISED

Use: A blackcurrant flavoured analgesic liquid for general pain relief, containing 120 mg of paracetamol in every 5 ml, and promethazine hydrochloride, an antihistamine.

Dose: Take a maximum of four doses in 24 hours. Children (1-6 years) should be given 10 ml every four hours if required. Children (6-12 years) should be given 20 ml every four hours. This treatment is not recommended for babies under one year. The product is also available in sugar and colour-free versions.

MELTUS COUGH ELIXIR – See under Adult Meltus Cough Elixir

MENTHOLAIR

Use: An aromatic bath vapour for relieving sinusitis congestion, containing aromatic decongestants.

Dose: One measure should be added to bath water.

MENTHOLATUM

Use: An ointment for the treatment of muscular aches and pains, containing rubefacients and a salicylate, an aspirin derivative.

Dose: The product should be applied to the affected area 2-3 times a day. This treatment is not recommended for children under one year.

MEROCAINE LOZENGES

Use: Lozenges for relieving sore throats, containing cetylypridium, an antibacterial and benzocaine, an anaesthetic.

Dose: One lozenge should be dissolved in the mouth every two hours. Take a maximum of eight pastilles in 24 hours. This treatment is not recommended for children under 12 years.

MEROCETS LOZENGES

Use: Lozenges for relieving sore throats, containing cetylp yearidium, an antibacterial.

Dose: One lozenge should be dissolved in the mouth every three hours or as required. This treatment is not recommended for children under six years. The product is also available as a mouthwash.

MEROTHOL LOZENGES
Use: Lozenges for relieving sore throats, containing cetylp yearidium, an antibacterial with menthol and eucalyptus.
Dose: One lozenge should be dissolved in the mouth every three hours or as required. This treatment is not recommended for children under the age of six years.

METANIUM OINTMENT
Use: An ointment for relieving nappy rash, containing titanium salts, and an astringent.
Dose: The ointment should be applied to clean dry skin at each nappy change.

METATONE
Use: A liquid remedy for alleviating fatigue, containing calcium, potassium, sodium, manganese and vitamin B1.
Dose: Adults should take 5-10 ml 2-3 times a day. Children (6-12 years) should be given 5 ml two to three times a day. This treatment is not recommended for children under six years.

METED SHAMPOO
Use: A medicated shampoo for the treatment of dandruff, containing salicylic acid.
Dose: Should be used as a shampoo twice a week.

MICRALAX MICRO-ENEMA
Use: Disposable plastic tube with nozzle in which 5 ml of a colourless viscous liquid contains sodium citrate 9.0%, sodium alkylsulphoacetate 0.9% with sorbic acid, glycerin, sorbitol and purified water, for the temporary relief of constipation.
Dose: Suitable for adults and children over 3 years. Administer the contents of one microenema rectally, inserting the full length of the nozzle. Not for use in patients with inflammatory disease.

MIGRALEVE 1 (PINK)
Use: Pink tablets for relieving migraines that are accompanied by nausea and vomiting. The tablets contain 500 mg of paracetamol, 8 mg of codeine phosphate and 6.25 mg of buclizine hydrochloride, a sedative antihistamine.
Dose: Adults should take two tablets as soon as an attack is about to start. Take a maximum of two tablets in 24 hours. Children (10-14 years) should be given no more than one tablet in 24 hours. This treatment is not recommended for children under 10 years.

MIGRALEVE 2 (YELLOW)

Use: Yellow tablets that can be taken in the later stages of a migraine attack after Migraleve 1 has been taken. They contain 500 mg of paracetamol and 8 mg of codeine phosphate.

Dose: Adults should take two tablets every four hours. Take a maximum of six tablets in 24 hours. Children (10-14 years) should be given one tablet every four hours, with a maximum of three tablets in 24 hours. This treatment is not suitable for children under 10 years.

MIGRALEVE DUO

Use: Pink and yellow tablets for a complete migraine attack. The pink tablet contains 500 mg of paracetamol, 8 mg of codeine phosphate and 6.25 mg of buclizine hydrochloride (a sedative antihistamine). The yellow tablet contains 500 mg of paracetamol and 8 mg of codeine phosphate.

Dose: Adults should take two pink tablets at the beginning of an attack. If required later, two yellow tablets should be taken every four hours. Take a maximum of two pink and six yellow tablets in 24 hours. Children (10-14 years) should be given one pink tablet at the beginning of an attack. If required later, one yellow tablet can be given every four hours, with no more than one pink tablet and three yellow tablets in 24 hours. This treatment is not recommended for children under the age of 10 years.

MILK OF MAGNESIA

Use: A liquid remedy for relieving indigestion, heartburn, upset stomachs and constipation. It contains magnesium hydroxide, an osmotic laxative.

Dose: Adults should take 30-45 ml on retiring. Children over three years should be given 5-10 ml at bedtime. This treatment is not recommended for children under three years.

MIL-PAR

Use: A liquid remedy for easing constipation, containing magnesium sulphate, an osmotic laxative, and liquid paraffin, which helps to soften the stools.

Dose: Adults should take 15-30 ml a day. Children over three years should be given 5-15 ml a day, depending on age. Read the label for the correct dosage. This treatment is not recommended for children under three years of age.

MINADEX TONIC

Use: A liquid treatment for alleviating fatigue, containing the vitamins A and D3, calcium, copper, iron, magnesium and potassium.

Dose: Adults should take 10 ml, three times a day. Children (3-12 years) should be given 5 mls, three times a day. Children

(6 months-3 years) should be given 5 ml twice a day. This treatment is not recommended for children under six years.

MINTEC

Use: Capsules for the treatment of irritable bowel syndrome, containing peppermint oil, which can help to calm intestinal spasms.
Dose: One capsule should be taken three times a day just before a meal, swallowed whole to prevent the peppermint oil irritating the throat. This treatment is not recommended for children under 12 years.

MOLCER EAR DROPS

Use: Ear drops containing softening ingredients for the removal of earwax.
Dose: The ear should be filled with the drops and plugged with cotton wool. The treatment should be repeated for two nights, and then clear out the ear.

MONPHYTOL PAINT

Use: A liquid treatment for athlete's foot, containing a mixture of antifungals.
Dose: The liquid should be applied to the affected area twice a day. The treatment should be repeated until the infection has cleared.

MOORLAND

Use: Antacid tablets for relieving indigestion and heartburn.
Dose: Two tablets should be dissolved in the mouth as required, after meals and at bedtime. This treatment is not recommended for children under six years.

MORHULIN OINTMENT

Use: An emollient ointment relieving the discomfort of eczema, dermatitis and nappy rash, containing cod liver oil and zinc oxide, an astringent and an antiseptic.
Dose: The ointment should be applied to the affected area thinly. For nappy rash, apply after washing and drying baby's bottom.

MOTILIUM 10

Use: Tablets for easing digestive discomfort, containing domperidone, an ingredient to help speed up the digestive system.
Dose: One tablet should be taken three times a day and at night if required. This treatment is not recommended for children under 16 years.

MOVELAT RELIEF CREAM

Use: A cream for the treatment of muscular aches and pains, containing salicylic acid, an aspirin derivative, and an ingredient for reducing swelling.

Dose: The product should be applied to the affected area up to four times a day. This treatment is not recommended for children under 12 years. The product is also available as a gel.

MU-CRON

Use: A tablet for easing the congestion of colds and catarrh, containing paracetamol and phenylpropanolamine, a decongestant.

Dose: One tablet can be taken up to four times a day, allowing four hours between doses. Take a maximum of four tablets in 24 hours. This treatment is not recommended for children under 12 years.

MULTI-ACTION ACTIFIED TABLETS

Use: White tablets for the treatment of allergic rhinitis and colds. Contains triprolidine hydrochloride and pseudoephedrine hydrochloride.

Dose: Adults and children over 12 should take one tablet every 4-6 hours up to four times a day. May cause drowsiness. Not to be used with MAOIs or for two weeks after completion of MAOI therapy. Not for use in severe hypertension or coronary heart disease, renal or hepatic impairment. Caution in diabetes, glaucoma, prostatic enlargement or hyperthyroidism.

MYCIL ATHLETE'S FOOT SPRAY

Use: A powder in a spray form for the treatment of athlete's foot. It contains tolnaftate, an antifungal ingredient.

Dose: The product should be applied morning and evening until the symptoms clear, and continued for a further seven days.

MYCIL GOLD CLOTRIMAZOLE

Use: A cream treatment for athlete's foot, containing the antifungal ingredient, clotrimazole.

Dose: The cream should be applied thinly to clean, dry feet, two to three times a day for up to one month.

MYCIL OINTMENT

Use: An ointment treatment for athlete's foot, containing the antifungal ingredient tolnaftate.

Dose: The product should be applied to the affected part morning and evening and continued for a further seven days once the infection has cleared.

MYCIL POWDER

Use: A powder treatment for athlete's foot, containing the antifungal ingredient tolnaftate.

Dose: The powder should be sprinkled over the affected area morning and evening. Treatment should be continued for a further seven days after the infection has cleared.

MYCOTA CREAM

Use: A cream treatment for athlete's foot, containing undecenoic acid, an antifungal ingredient.

Dose: Apply the cream to clean, dry skin. The treatment should be continued for a further seven days after the infection has cleared.

MYCOTA POWDER

Use: A powder for the treatment of athlete's foot. It contains undecenoic acid and zinc undecenoate, both antifungal ingredients.

Dose: Sprinkle the powder over the affected area morning and evening. The treatment should be continued for a further seven days after the infection has cleared up. This product is also available in spray form.

NASCIODINE

Use: A cream treatment for relieving muscular aches and pains, containing rubefacients and a salicylate, an aspirin derivative.

Dose: The cream should be massaged into the affected area 2-3 times a day. This treatment is not recommended for children under six years.

NASOBEC HAYFEVER

Use: A nasal spray for easing hayfever symptoms. The spray contains beclomethasone, a corticosteroid.

Dose: Two sprays should be directed into each nostril, with a maximum of eight sprays in 24 hours. This treatment is not recommended for children under 12 years.

NEO BABY CREAM

Use: A cream for the treatment of nappy rash, containing cetrimide and benzalkonium, both antiseptics.

Dose: The product should be applied to clean dry skin as required.

NEO BABY MIXTURE

Use: A liquid remedy for relieving infant wind and colic, containing sodium bicarbonate, an antacid, dill oil and ginger.

Dose: 2.5-15 ml, three times a day, according to age. Check the label for the correct dosage.

NERICUR

Use: A gel available in two strengths for the treatment of spots and acne, containing benzoyl peroxide.

Dose: The gel should be applied once a day to clean dry skin. Use the lower strength version first and progress to the stronger version if necessary. This treatment is not recommended for children under the age of 15 years.

NICORETTE

Use: A treatment for nicotine dependence (for those who smoke less than 20 cigarettes a day) in the form of chewing gum, containing 2 mg of nicotine per gum piece.

Dose: One piece of gum should be chewed for 30 minutes. Take a maximum of 15 pieces in 24 hours. After three months the dosage should be reduced. Nicorette Plus is also available, containing 4 mg of nicotine per piece of gum.

NICORETTE INHALER

Use: These are inhalable cartridges for nicotine dependence (for those who smoke more than 20 cigarettes a day). One cartridge contains 10 mg of nicotine.

Dose: The cartridge should be fixed into the inhaler and sucked when an urge to have a cigarette arises. Use a minimum of 12 cartridges in 24 hours. The amount should be reduced over three months.

NICORETTE PATCH

Use: A skin patch for treating nicotine dependence.

Dose: These patches are available in 5 mg, 10 mg and 15 mg strengths. One patch should be applied to the arm on waking and removed 16 hours later. The dose should be reduced gradually by using lower dosage patches.

NICOTINELL CHEWING GUM

Use: A chewing gum for treating nicotine dependence. Each piece of gum contains 2 mg of nicotine.

Dose: 8-12 pieces of gum should be chewed a day. Take a maximum of 25 pieces in 24 hours. The number of pieces of gum should be reduced gradually over a three-month period. The product is also available in 4 mg pieces.

NICOTINELL TTS (PATCH)

Use: A skin patch treatment for reducing nicotine dependence.

Dose: There are three strength doses available according to cigarette consumption. The dosage should be reduced gradually over a three-month period.

NIGHT NURSE

Use: A liquid remedy for easing cold and flu symptoms at night, containing paracetamol, promethazine, an antihistamine and dextromethorphan, a cough suppressant.

Dose: Adults should take 20 ml just before retiring. Children (6-12 years) should be given 10 ml just before retiring. This treatment is not recommended for children under six years.

NIZORAL DANDRUFF SHAMPOO
Use: A medicated shampoo for the treatment of dandruff, containing ketoconazole.
Dose: Should be used as a shampoo, left in for 2-3 minutes and then rinsed out. It should be used twice a week for 2-4 weeks, reducing use to once every 1-2 weeks as a preventive measure.

NOSTROLIN
Use: Ointment for the relief from blocked noses. Soothes nostrils, nose and upper lip. Contains menthol, eucalyptol and geranium oil.
Dose: Apply two or three times a day. For external use only.

NOXACORN
Use: A liquid for the treatment of corns and calluses, containing salicylic acid.
Dose: The liquid should be applied every night to the affected area, for 3-6 nights. This treatment is not recommended for children under six years.

NULACIN TABLETS
Use: Antacid tablets for relieving indigestion, heartburn and general digestive discomfort.
Dose: One tablet should be sucked slowly as required. Take a maximum of eight tablets in 24 hours. This treatment is not recommended for children under 12 years.

NUPERCAINAL
Use: An ointment treatment for piles, containing cinchocaine, a mild local anaesthetic.
Dose: The ointment should be applied sparingly to the affected area up to three times a day. This treatment is not recommended for children under 12 years.

NUROFEN
Use: Analgesic tablets for pain relief, containing 200 mg of ibuprofen.
Dose: Two tablets should be taken initially, and a further 1-2 tablets every four hours if required. Take a maximum of six tablets in 24 hours. This treatment is not recommended for children under 12 years.

NUROFEN ADVANCE
Use: Analgesic tablets for general pain relief, containing 200 mg of

ibuprofen.

Dose: Two tablets should be taken initially, and a further 1-2 tablets every 4-6 hours if required. Take a maximum of six tablets in 24 hrs. This treatment is not recommended for children under 12 years.

NUROFEN COLD AND FLU

Use: Tablets for relieving the symptoms of cold and flu. Each tablet contains ibuprofen and pseudoephedrine, a decongestant.

Dose: Two tablets should be taken initially, followed by 1-2 tablets every four hours if required. Take a maximum of six tablets in 24 hours. This treatment is not recommended for children under 12 years.

NUROFEN FOR CHILDREN

Use: An orange flavoured analgesic liquid for general pain relief, which is sugar- and colour-free, containing 100 mg of ibuprofen in every 5 ml.

Dose: Take a maximum of four doses in 24 hours. Babies (6-12 months) should be given 2.5 ml up to three times in 24 hours. Babies (1-2 years) should be given 2.5 ml every four hours if required. Children (3-7 years) should be given 5 ml every four hours. Children (8-12 years) should be given 10 ml every four hours. This treatment is not recommended for babies under six months.

NUROFEN 400

Use: Analgesic tablets for general pain relief, containing 400 mg of ibuprofen.

Dose: One tablet should be taken initially, followed by one tablet every four hours if required. Take a maximum of three tablets in 24 hours. This treatment is not recommended for children under 12 years.

NUROFEN MICRO-GRANULES

Use: Effervescent analgesic granules for general pain relief. Each sachet contains 400 mg of ibuprofen.

Dose: One sachet should be dissolved in water and a further sachet can be taken every four hours if required. Take a maximum of three sachets in 24 hours. This treatment is not recommended for children under 12 years.

NUROFEN PLUS

Use: Analgesic tablets for general pain relief containing 200 mg of ibuprofen and 12.5 mg of codeine phosphate.

Dose: Two tablets should be taken initially, and then 1-2 tablets every 4-6 hours if required. Take a maximum of six tablets in 24 hours. This treatment is not recommended for children under 12 years.

NURSE HARVEY'S GRIPE MIXTURE

Use: A liquid remedy for relieving infant colic and wind, containing sodium bicarbonate, an antacid, and dill oil and caraway oil.

Dose: 5-10 ml should be given according to age, after or during feeds. Give a maximum of six doses in 24 hours. This treatment is not recommended for babies under one month.

NURSE SYKES BRONCHIAL BALSAM

Use: A liquid remedy for relieving coughs, containing guaiphenesin, an expectorant.

Dose: 5-10 ml should be taken every four hours and at bedtime. This treatment is not recommended for children under 12 years.

NURSE SYKES POWDERS

Use: An analgesic powder for general pain relief, containing 165.3 mg of aspirin, 120 mg of paracetamol, and caffeine.

Dose: One powder should be dissolved in water and taken every four hours. Take a maximum of six powders in 24 hours. This treatment is not recommended for children under 12 years.

NYLAX

Use: A constipation remedy in the form of tablets. Each tablet contains senna, which is a stimulant laxative.

Dose: Adults should take two tablets on retiring. Children (5-12 years) should be given one tablet at bedtime. This treatment is not recommended for children under five years.

NYTOL

Use: A tablet remedy for insomnia, containing diphenhydramine, an antihistamine.

Dose: Two tablets should be taken 20 minutes before retiring. This treatment is not recommended for children under 16 years.

OCCLUSAL

Use: A liquid treatment for the removal of warts and verrucae, containing salicylic acid.

Dose: The product should be applied to the wart or verruca and allowed to dry. The treatment should be repeated daily. This treatment is not recommended for children under six years, unless advised otherwise by a doctor.

OILATUM EMOLLIENT

Use: An emollient liquid for the treatment of eczema and dermatitis, containing various oils.

Dose: The liquid can be added to the bath water, or applied to the skin directly and rinsed off afterwards. The product is also available as shower gel and hand gel.

OILATUM JUNIOR FLARE UP
Use: An emollient liquid for treating the discomfort of eczema and dermatitis in children, containing a mixture of oils and antiseptics.
Dose: The liquid should be added to bath water.

OILATUM PLUS
Use: An emollient liquid for relieving the discomfort of skin disorders such as eczema and dermatitis, containing a mixture of oils and antiseptics.
Dose: The liquid should be added to bath water.

OPAS
Use: Antacid tablets for easing indigestion and heartburn, containing sodium.
Dose: 1-2 tablets should be taken after each meal, or as required. This treatment is not recommended for children under 12 years.

OPAZIMES
Use: Tablets to help stop diarrhoea, containing kaolin, morphine and belladonna.
Dose: Adults should chew or suck two tablets every four hours, with a maximum of eight tablets in 24 hours. Children over six years should chew or suck one tablet every four hours, with a maximum of four tablets in 24 hours. This treatment is not recommended for children under six years.

OPTICROM ALLERGY EYE DROPS
Use: Eye drops for relieving itchy eyes caused by hayfever, containing sodium cromoglycate, an anti-inflammatory.
Dose: 1-2 drops should be applied to each eye four times a day. This treatment is not recommended for children under five years.

OPTREX HAYFEVER ALLERGY EYE DROPS
Use: Eye drops for relieving itchy eyes caused by hayfever, containing sodium cromoglycate, an anti-inflammatory.
Dose: 1-2 drops should be applied to each eye four times a day. This treatment is not recommended for children under five years.

ORALDENE
Use: This is a mouthwash for the treatment of mouth infections, sore gums and bad breath. It contains hexetidine, an anti-microbial.
Dose: 15 ml of the mouthwash should be rinsed or gargled 2-3 times a day. The product should not be diluted or swallowed. This treatment is not recommended for children under 5 years.

ORUVAIL

Use: This is a gel for the treatment of muscular aches and pains, containing ketoprofen, a non-steroidal anti-inflammatory (NSAID).

Dose: The gel should be massaged into the affected area three times a day. This treatment is not recommended for children under 12 years.

OTEX EAR DROPS

Use: Ear drops for the removal of earwax, containing softening ingredients.

Dose: 5 drops of the liquid should be put into the ear once or twice a day, for 3-4 days until the wax loosens.

OTRADROPS ADULT FORMULA

Use: An aqueous solution containing xylometazoline hydrochloride for the treatment of nasal congestion associated with colds, hayfever and sinusitis.

Dose: Adults and children over 12 years should take 2-3 drops of solution in each nostril 2-3 times daily. Do not use continuously for more than seven days.

OTRADROPS CHILD FORMULA

Use: An aqueous solution containing xylometazoline hydrochloride for the treatment of nasal congestion associated with colds, hayfever and sinusitis.

Dose: Children 2-12 years should take 1-2 drops of solution in each nostril 2-3 times daily. Do not use continuously for more than seven days. Consult a doctor for infants under 2 years. Not for children under 3 months.

OTRIVINE-ANTISTIN

Use: Eye drops for hayfever sufferers, containing xylometazeline, a decongestant and antazoline, a topical antihistamine.

Dose: Adults should take 1-2 drops into the affected eye/s, 2-3 times a day. Children over five years should be given one drop 2-3 times a day. This treatment is not recommended for children under five years.

OVEX TABLETS

Use: Tablets for the treatment of intestinal worms, containing mebendazole, an anti-worm ingredient.

Dose: For threadworms one dose of one tablet should be taken. This should be repeated after two weeks if the infestation is still present. Treatment is not recommended for children under two years.

OXY 5

Use: This is a lotion for the treatment of spots and acne, containing benzoyl peroxide.

Dose: The lotion should be applied once a day for one week. If no irritation occurs, it can be applied twice a day. The lower dose should be used first, progressing to the stronger version if required – Oxy 10. This treatment is not recommended for children under 15 years.

PACIFENE

Use: Analgesic tablets for general pain relief, containing 200 mg of ibuprofen.

Dose: 1-2 tablets should be taken three times a day. Take a maximum of six tablets in 24 hours. This treatment is not recommended for children under 12 years.

PACIFENE MAXIMUM STRENGTH

Use: Analgesic tablets for general pain relief, containing 400 mg of ibuprofen.

Dose: One tablet should be taken every four hours. Take a maximum of three tablets in 24 hours. This treatment is not recommended for children under 12 years.

PANADEINE

Use: Analgesic tablets for general pain relief, containing 500 mg of paracetamol and 8mg of codeine phosphate.

Dose: Adults should take two tablets up to four times a day. Take a maximum of eight tablets in 24 hours. Children (7-12 years) should be given half to one tablet every four hours. A maximum of four tablets should be taken in 24 hours. This treatment is not recommended for children under seven years.

PANADOL

Use: Analgesic tablets for general pain relief, containing 500 mg of paracetamol.

Dose: Adults should take two tablets every four hours. Take a maximum of eight tablets in 24 hours. Children (6-12 years) should be given half to one tablet every four hours, with a maximum of four tablets in 24 hours. This treatment is not recommended for children under six years.

PANADOL CAPSULES

Use: Analgesic capsules for general pain relief, containing 500 mg of paracetamol.

Dose: Two capsules should be taken every four hours if required. Take a maximum of eight capsules in 24 hours. This treatment is not recommended for children under 12 years.

PANADOL EXTRA

Use: Analgesic tablets for general pain relief containing 500 mg of paracetamol, and caffeine.

Dose: Two tablets can be taken every four hours if required. Take a maximum of eight tablets in 24 hours. This treatment is not recommended for children under 12 years.

PANADOL EXTRA SOLUBLE

Use: Effervescent analgesic tablets for general pain relief, containing 500 mg of paracetamol, and caffeine.

Dose: Two tablets should be dissolved in water every four hours if required. Take a maximum of eight tablets in 24 hours. This treatment is not recommended for children under 12 years.

PANADOL NIGHT

Use: Analgesic capsules for general pain relief, containing 500 mg of paracetamol, and diphendydramine, an antihistamine.

Dose: Two tablets should be taken 20 minutes before retiring. This treatment is not recommended for children under 12 years.

PANADOL SOLUBLE

Use: An effervescent tablet for general pain relief, containing 500 mg of paracetamol.

Dose: Adults should take two tablets dissolved in water every four hours if required. Take a maximum of eight tablets in 24 hours. Children (6-12 years) should be given half to one tablet dissolved in water every four hours if required, with a maximum of four tablets in 24 hours. This treatment is not recommended for children under six years.

PANADOL ULTRA

Use: Analgesic tablets for general pain relief, containing 500 mg of paracetamol and 12.8 mg of codeine phosphate.

Dose: Two tablets should be taken up to four times a day if required. Take a maximum of four tablets in 24 hours. This treatment is not recommended for children under 12 years.

PANOXYL ACNEGEL

Use: This is a gel for the treatment of acne and spots, available in two strengths, containing benzoyl peroxide.

Dose: The product should be applied to clean skin once a day, using the lower strength version first and then progressing to the higher strength version if necessary. This treatment is not recommended for children under 15 years.

PANOXYL AQUAGEL
Use: This is a gel available in three strengths for the treatment of acne and spots.
Dose: The product should be applied to clean skin once a day using the lower strength first, then progressing to the stronger version if required. This treatment is not recommended for children under 15 years.

PANOXYL 5 CREAM
Use: A cream for the treatment of acne and spots, containing benzoyl peroxide.
Dose: The product should be applied to clean skin once a day. This treatment is not recommended for children under 15 years.

PANOXYL LOTION
Use: This is a lotion for the treatment of acne and spots, available in two strengths. It contains benzoyl peroxide.
Dose: The product should be applied to clean skin once a day, using the lower dose first, then progressing to the higher strength version if required. This treatment is not recommended for children under 15 years.

PANOXYL WASH
Use: This is a wash for the treatment of acne and spots, containing benzoyl peroxide.
Dose: The wash should be applied to wet skin, rinsed with alternate warm and cold water and patted dry. Use once a day in the morning. This treatment is not recommended for children under 15 years.

PAPULEX
Use: This is a gel for the treatment of spots and acne, containing nicotinamide, an anti-inflammatory.
Dose: The gel should be applied twice a day after washing. This should be reduced to once every other day if there is an adverse skin reaction. This treatment is not recommended for children under 15 years.

PARACETS
Use: Analgesic tablets for general pain relief, containing 500 mg of paracetamol.
Dose: Adults should take two tablets up to four times a day if required. Take a maximum of eight tablets in 24 hours. Children (6-12 years) should be given half to one tablet up to four times a day, with a maximum of four tablets in 24 hours. This treatment is not recommended for children under six years.

PARACETS CAPSULES
Use: Analgesic capsules for general pain relief, containing 500 mg of paracetamol.
Dose: Adults should take 1-2 capsules every six hours. Take a maximum of eight capsules in 24 hours. Children (6-12 years) should be given one capsule every six hours. This treatment is not recommended for children under six years.

PARACLEAR
Use: Effervescent analgesic tablets for general pain relief, containing 500 mg of paracetamol.
Dose: Adults should take 1-2 tablets dissolved in water every four hours. Take a maximum of eight tablets in 24 hours. Children (6-12 years) should be given one tablet every four hours. Take a maximum of four tablets in 24 hours. This treatment is not recommended for children under six years.

PARACLEAR EXTRA STRENGTH
Use: Analgesic tablets for general pain relief, containing 500 mg of paracetamol, and caffeine.
Dose: 1-2 tablets should be taken every 4-6 hours. Take a maximum of eight tablets in 24 hours. This treatment is not recommended for children under 12 years.

PARACODOL
Use: Analgesic capsules for general pain relief, containing 500 mg of paracetamol and 8 mg of codeine phosphate.
Dose: 1-2 capsules should be taken every four to six hours. Take a maximum of eight capsules in 24 hours. This treatment is not recommended for children under 12 years. The product is also available in soluble tablet form.

PARAMOL
Use: Analgesic tablets for general pain relief, containing 500 mg of paracetamol and 7.46 mg dihydrocodeine tartrate.
Dose: 1-2 tablets should be taken during or after meals, every four to six hours as required. Take a maximum of eight tablets in 24 hours. This treatment is not recommended for children under 12 years.

PAVACOL D
Use: A sugar-free liquid remedy for relieving coughs, containing pholcodine, a cough suppressant.
Dose: Adults should take 5-10 ml four times a day if required. Children (1-12 years) should be given 2.5-5 ml three to five times a day according to age. Read the label for the correct dosage. This treatment

is not suitable for children under one year.

PAXIDORM TABLETS
Use: Tablets for insomnia, containing diphenhydramine, an antihistamine.
Dose: 1-2 tablets should be taken just before retiring. This treatment is not recommended for children under 16 years.

PENTRAX
Use: A medicated shampoo for the treatment of dandruff, containing coal tar.
Dose: The treatment should be used as an ordinary shampoo twice a week.

PEPCID AC
Use: Tablets for relieving general stomach discomfort, indigestion and heartburn, containing famotidine, a histamine H2 antagonist that helps reduce stomach acid.
Dose: One tablet should be taken one hour before eating. Take a maximum of two tablets in 24 hours. This treatment is not recommended for children under 16 years, and should not be taken for more than two weeks.

PEPTO-BISMOL
Use: A liquid remedy for relieving indigestion, heartburn and general stomach discomfort. The liquid contains bismuth, an ingredient to coat the stomach lining.
Dose: Adults should take 30 ml every 30 minutes to one hour. Children (10-14 years) should be given 20 ml every 30 minutes to one hour. Children (6-10 years) should be given 10 ml every 30 minutes to one hour. Children (3-6 years), up to eight doses in 24 hours. This treatment is not recommended for children under three years.

PERVARYL
Use: A cream for the treatment of athlete's foot, containing econazole, an antifungal ingredient.
Dose: The cream should be applied twice a day for as long as it is needed. This product is also available in lotion and powder forms.

PHENERGAN
Use: Tablets for preventing travel sickness, containing promethazine, an antihistamine. The tablets are available in two strengths, 10 mg and 25 mg.
Dose: Adults and children over 10 years should take one to two 10 mg tablets, or one 25 mg tablet, the night before the journey. The dose should be repeated after six to eight hours if necessary. Children

(5-10 years) should be given one 10 mg tablet the night before the journey, and then again 6-8 hours later if necessary. The 25 mg tablets are not suitable for children under 10 years. A liquid version is available for younger children (2-5 years). This treatment is not recommended for children under two years.

PHENERGAN NIGHTIME
Use: A tablet remedy for insomnia, containing promethazine, an antihistamine.
Dose: Two tablets should be taken at night. This treatment is not recommended for children under 16 years.

PHENSEDYL PLUS LINCTUS
Use: A liquid remedy for the treatment of coughs, containing promethazine, an antihistamine, pholcodine, a cough suppressant and pseudoephedrine, a decongestant.
Dose: 5-10 ml should be taken 3-4 times a day. This treatment is not recommended for children under 12 years.

PHENSIC
Use: Analgesic tablets for general pain relief, containing 325 mg of aspirin and 22 mg of caffeine.
Dose: Two tablets should be taken every 3-4 hours as required. Take a maximum of 12 tablets in 24 hours. This treatment is not recommended for children under 12 years.

PICKLE'S OINTMENT
Use: An ointment for the treatment of corns and calluses, containing salicylic acid.
Dose: The product should be applied to the affected area at night for four nights. The skin should be allowed to fall off before reapplying the ointment.

PIRITON ALLERGY TABLETS
Use: A tablet for relieving hayfever symptoms, containing chlorpheniramine, an antihistamine.
Dose: Adults should take one tablet every 4-6 hours, with a maximum of six tablets in 24 hours. Children (6-12 years) should be given half a tablet every 4-6 hours, with a maximum of three tablets in 24 hours. This treatment is not recommended for children under six years.

PIRITON SYRUP
Use: A liquid remedy for relieving hayfever symptoms, containing chlorpheniramine, an antihistamine.
Dose: Adults should take 10 ml every 4-6 hours. Children (1-12 years) should be given 2.5-5 ml, according to age. Read the label for the

correct dosage. This treatment is not recommended for babies under one year.

PLACIDEX SYRUP
Use: An analgesic liquid for general pain relief, containing 120 mg of paracetamol in every 5 ml.
Dose: A maximum of four doses can be given in 24 hours. Babies (3-12 months) should be given 2.5-5 ml every four hours if required. This treatment is not recommended for babies under three months unless advised otherwise by a doctor.

POLYTAR AF
Use: A liquid for the treatment of dandruff, containing peanut oil, zinc pyithione and coal tar.
Dose: The liquid should be massaged into the hair and scalp and left in for 2-3 minutes before rinsing out. Use 2-3 times a week.

POLYTAR EMOLLIENT
Use: A medicated treatment for dandruff, containing coal tar and peanut oil.
Dose: 2-4 capfuls should be added into a shallow bath.

POLYTAR LIQUID
Use: A liquid treatment for dandruff, containing coal tar and peanut oil.
Dose: The lotion should be applied to wet hair, massaged into the scalp and rinsed out. This should be carried out twice. The lotion should be used once or twice a week.

POLYTAR PLUS
Use: A liquid treatment for dandruff, containing coal tar, peanut oil and a hair conditioner.
Dose: The lotion should be applied to wet hair, massaged into the scalp and rinsed out. This should be carried out twice. The lotion should be used one to two times a week.

PREPARATION H OINTMENT
Use: An ointment for the treatment of piles, containing shark oil, a skin protectant.
Dose: The ointment should be applied morning and evening and after each bowel movement. This treatment is not recommended for children under 12 years. The product is also available in suppository form.

PR FREEZE SPRAY
Use: A spray for relieving muscular pain, containing cooling

ingredients.

Dose: The spray should be applied to the affected area up to three times a day. This treatment is not recommended for children under six years.

PR HEAT SPRAY

Use: A spray for the treatment of muscular aches and pains, containing rubefacients and a salicylate, an aspirin derivative.

Dose: The product should be applied to the affected area twice a day. This treatment is not recommended for children under five years.

PRIODERM CREAM SHAMPOO

Use: A shampoo for the treatment of head lice, containing malathion.

Dose: The treatment should be shampooed into the hair and left for five minutes, then rinsed out. This should be carried out twice. Repeat this twice more at three-day intervals. The lotion can be also used for treating pubic lice. This treatment is not recommended for babies under six months.

PRIODERM LOTION

Use: A lotion for the treatment of lice and scabies, containing malathion and alcohol.

Dose: For head or pubic lice, the lotion should be applied to the affected area and left to dry for at least two hours, but preferably for 12 hours if possible. The treatment should then be washed off and the hair combed out while still wet. For scabies the lotion should be applied to the whole body and left on for 24 hours before washing off. This treatment is not recommended for babies under six months.

PRIPSEN MEBENDAZOLE TABLETS

Use: Tablets for removing intestinal worms, containing mebendazole, an anti-worm ingredient.

Dose: For threadworms one dose of one tablet should be taken. This can be repeated after two weeks if the infestation is still present. This treatment is not recommended for children under two years.

PRIPSEN PIPERAZINE CITRATE ELIXIR

Use: A liquid remedy for the removal of intestinal worms, containing piperazine citrate, an anti-worm ingredient.

Dose: For threadworms, adults should take 15 ml a day for seven days. This can be repeated after a seven-day interval if required. Children should be given 5-10 ml a day, depending on age, for seven days. The treatment should be repeated for a further seven days after a seven-day interval.

For roundworms, adults should take one single 30 ml dose, and then another 30 ml dose after 14 days. Children should be given 10-25 ml dose, according to age, and then another dose after 14 days. This treatment is not recommended for babies under one year unless advised otherwise by a doctor.

PRIPSEN PIPERAZINE PHOSPHATE POWDER

Use: A powder treatment for the removal of intestinal worms, containing piperazine phosphate, an anti-worm ingredient.

Dose: For threadworms and roundworms, adults and children over six years should take one sachet dissolved in a measured quantity of milk. Adults should take at bed-time, and children in the morning. Children (1-6 years) should be given 5 ml of the sachet contents in the morning. For threadworms, a repeat dose should be taken 14 days after the first dose. For roundworms, additional doses can be taken each month to avoid re-infestation. This treatment is not recommended for babies under one year unless advised otherwise by a doctor.

PROFLEX

Use: An analgesic for general pain relief containing 200 mg of ibuprofen.

Dose: 1-2 capsules to be taken three times a day. Take a maximum of six capsules in 24 hours. The treatment is not recommended for children under 12 years.

PROFLEX PAIN RELIEF

Use: A cream for the treatment of muscular pains, containing ibuprofen, a non-steroidal anti-inflammatory (NSAID).

Dose: The cream should be massaged into the affected area 3-4 times a day. This treatment is not recommended for children under 12 years.

PROFLEX SUSTAINED RELIEF CAPSULES

Use: Analgesic capsules for general pain relief, containing 300 mg of ibuprofen.

Dose: Two capsules should be taken twice a day. Take a maximum of four in 24 hours. This treatment is not recommended for children under 12 years.

PROPAIN

Use: Analgesic tablets for general pain relief, containing 400 mg of paracetamol, 10 mg of codeine phosphate, 5 mg of diphenhydramine, and caffeine.

Dose: 1-2 tablets should be taken every four hours. Take a maximum of 10 tablets in 24 hours. This treatment is not recommended for children under 12 years.

PSORIGEL

Use: A gel for the treatment of eczema and dermatitis, containing coal tar.

Dose: The gel should be rubbed into the affected area and allowed to dry, once or twice a day.

PSORIN OINTMENT
Use: An ointment for the topical treatment of sub-acute and chronic (stable) psoriasis. Contains dithranol, coal tar and salicylic acid.
Dose: Apply a small quantity to the affected areas morning and evening for 7 days. If no redness occurs, it may then be applied more liberally twice daily. Avoid direct exposure to sunlight unless specifically directed by a doctor. Avoid contact with eyes. For external use only.

PULMO BAILLY
Use: A liquid remedy for relieving coughs, containing guaicol, an expectorant and codeine, a cough suppressant.
Dose: Adults should take up to 10 ml diluted in water, before food. Take a maximum of three doses in 24 hours. Children (5-15 years) should be given 5 ml. This treatment is not recommended for children under five years.

PYALVEX
Use: A liquid treatment for mouth ulcers, containing salicylic acid, an analgesic.
Dose: The liquid should be brushed onto the affected area 3-4 times a day. This treatment is not recommended for children under 12 years.

QUELLADA-M CREAM SHAMPOO
Use: A shampoo for the treatment for lice and scabies, containing malathion.
Dose: The shampoo should be applied to dry hair and scalp, and to the pubic area if necessary, left for four minutes, then lathered and rinsed off. This treatment is not recommended for babies under six months.

QUELLA-M LOTION
Use: A lotion for the treatment of lice and scabies, containing malathion and alcohol.
Dose: For head or pubic lice, the lotion should be applied to the affected area and left to dry for 2-12 hours. It should then be washed off and the hair combed out while wet. For scabies, the lotion should be applied to the whole body and left on for 24 hours before washing off. This treatment is not recommended for babies under six months.

QUINODERM CREAM
Use: A cream for the treatment of acne and spots available in two strengths, containing benzoyl peroxide.
Dose: The cream should be massaged into the affected area once to

three times a day, starting with the lower dose version and progressing to the stronger dose version if required. This treatment is not recommended for children under 15 years. The product is available as a lotion, gel and face wash.

QUINOPED CREAM

Use: This is a cream for the treatment of athlete's foot, containing benzoyl peroxide.
Dose: The cream should be massaged into the affected part twice a day.

RALGEX IBUTOP GEL

Use: A gel for the treatment of muscular aches and pains, containing a non-steroidal anti-inflammatory (NSAID).
Dose: The gel should be applied to the affected area three to four times a day, allowing at least four hours between applications. It should not be used more than four times in 24 hours. This treatment is not recommended for children under 12 years.

RADIAN-B HEAT SPRAY

Use: A spray for relieving muscular aches and pains, containing rubefacients and a salicylate, an aspirin derivative.
Dose: The product should be sprayed onto the affected area, and a second dose applied 15 minutes later. This can be repeated up to three times a day if required. The number of applications should be reduced as symptoms subside. This treatment is not recommended for children under six years. The product is also available as a lotion.

RADIAN-B IBUPROFEN GEL

Use: A gel for the treatment of muscular aches and pains, containing ibuprofen, a non-steroidal anti-inflammatory (NSAID).
Dose: The product should be applied to the affected area, and used every four hours if necessary, with a maximum of four applications in 24 hours. This treatment is not recommended for children under 14 years.

RALGEX CREAM

Use: A cream for alleviating muscular aches and pains, containing rubefacients and a salicylate, an aspirin derivative.
Dose: The cream should be applied to the affected area up to four times a day. This treatment is not recommended for children under 12 years.

RALGEX FREEZE SPRAY

Use: A cooling spray for relieving muscle pain, containing a salicylate, an aspirin derivative.

Dose: The product should be applied to the affected area up to four times a day. This treatment is not recommended for children under five years.

RALGEX HEAT SPRAY

Use: A spray for relieving muscular pain, containing rubefacients and a salicylate, an aspirin derivative.

Dose: Two or three short bursts of spray should be applied to the affected area every two hours if required, no more than four times a day. This treatment is not recommended for children under five years.

RALGEX STICK

Use: An embrocation stick for relieving muscular aches and pains, containing rubefacients and a salicylate, an aspirin derivative.

Dose: The product should be applied to the affected area as required. It should not be massaged or rubbed in. This treatment is not recommended for children.

RANZAC

Use: Tablets to relieve burning sensation in the stomach and chest caused by heartburn, indigestion, acid indigestion and hyperacidity. Tablets contain ranitide hydrochloride.

Dose: Adults should swallow one tablet as soon as symptoms present. Do not take more than 2 tablets in 24 hours. Do not take for more than 6 days without the advice of a doctor or pharmacist. Not to be given to children under 16 years.

RAP-EZE

Use: Antacid tablets for relieving indigestion and heartburn.

Dose: Two tablets should be chewed or sucked as required. Take a maximum of 16 tablets in 24 hours. This treatment is not recommended for children under 12 years.

RAPPELL

Use: Head louse repellent pump spray containing piperonal.

Dose: Use daily as a preventative during periods of high risk infection.

REGULAN

Use: A powder treatment for relieving constipation and irritable bowel syndrome. The powders consist of ispaghula husk, a bulk forming laxative.

Dose: Adults should take one sachet dissolved in water 1-3 times a day. Children (6-12 years) should be given half to one level teaspoonful dissolved in water 1-3 times a day. The powder should be taken with plenty of fluid and not before bedtime. This treatment is not recommended for children under six years. The product is also available in several flavours.

REGULOSE
Use: A liquid remedy for relieving constipation, containing lactulose, an osmotic laxative.
Dose: Adults and children over 12 years should take 15-30 ml daily for the first two or three days, reducing the dose to 10-15 ml daily thereafter. Children under 12 years should be given 10-25 ml for the first few days, reducing the dose to 5-15 ml thereafter.

REHIDRAT
Use: Powders to help replace the salts, minerals and water lost from the body during an attack of diarrhoea.
Dose: One sachet should be dissolved in a measured quantity of fluid (see pack for instructions) and taken after every loose bowel movement. Breast-fed babies should be given this fluid in place of their usual feed, but discuss with a doctor prior to use.

RELAXYL
Use: Capsules for relieving irritable bowel syndrome, containing alverine, an ingredient that helps control intestinal spasms.
Dose: 1-2 capsules should be taken up to three times a day. This treatment is not recommended for children under 12 years.

RELCOFEN
Use: Analgesic tablets for general pain relief, containing 200mg of ibuprofen.
Dose: 1-2 tablets should be taken three times a day. Take a maximum of six tablets in 24 hours. This treatment is not recommended for children under 12 years. A stronger version containing 400 mg of ibuprofen is also available.

REMEGEL ORIGINAL
Use: Square antacid tablets for easing indigestion and heartburn.
Dose: 1-2 squares should be chewed every hour. Take a maximum of 12 squares in 24 hours. This treatment is not recommended for children under 12 years. The product is available in several flavours.

RENNIE
Use: Antacid tablets for indigestion and heartburn.
Dose: Adults should suck or chew two tablets as required. Take a maximum of 16 tablets in 24 hours. Children (6-12 years) should be given one tablet as needed, with a maximum of eight tablets in 24 hours. This treatment is not recommended for children under six years. The product is available in several flavours.

RENNIE DEFLATINE
Use: Tablets to relieve feeling of bloatedness, fullness after food and

trapped wind; relief of symptoms of indigestion and associated heartburn. May be used throughout pregnancy. Tablets contain simethicone, calcium carbonate and heavy magnesium carbonate.

Dose: Adults and children should chew or suck one or two tablets as required as soon as any discomfort is felt. Do not take more than 16 tablets in 24 hours.

REPLENS
Use: A gel to provide lubrication and ease itchiness and irritation of the vagina, for post-menopausal women.
Dose: One dose of the gel should be applied into the vagina three times a week.

RESOLVE
Use: Relief of headache with upset stomach, particularly associated with over-indulgence. Effervescent granules in sachets, each containing paracetamol, anhydrous citric acid, sodium bicarbonate, potassium bicarbonate, sodium carbonate and vitamin C.
Dose: Adults and children over 12 years should take one sachet every 4 hours as required. Maximum of four sachets in 24 hours. Not to be given to children under 12 years. Do not take with other medicines containing paracetamol.

RHINOLAST HAYFEVER SPRAY
Use: A nasal spray for relieving hayfever symptoms, containing azelastin, an antihistamine.
Dose: One spray should be applied into each nostril twice a day. This treatment is not recommended for children under 12 years.

RINSTEAD ADULT GEL
Use: A gel for the treatment of mouth ulcers, containing benzocaine, an anaesthetic, and chloroxylenol, an antiseptic.
Dose: The gel should be applied to the affected area up to six times a day. This treatment is not recommended for young children. The product is also available in pastille form.

RINSTEAD TEETHING GEL
Use: A gel for relieving teething pain in babies, containing lignocaine, an anaesthetic, and an antiseptic.
Dose: The gel should be applied every three hours as required. This treatment is not recommended for babies under three months.

ROBITUSSIN CHESTY COUGH MEDICINE
Use: A liquid remedy for the treatment of coughs, containing guaiphenesin, an expectorant.
Dose: Adults should take 10 ml four times a day. Children (1-12 years)

should be 2.5-5 ml, according to age. Read the label for the correct dosage. This treatment is not recommended for children under one year.

ROBITUSSIN DRY COUGH
Use: A liquid remedy for the treatment of coughs, containing dextromethorphan, a cough suppressant.
Dose: Adults should take 10 ml four times a day. Children (6-12 years) should be given 5 ml four times a day. This treatment is not recommended for children under six years. A junior version is also available.

ROBITUSSIN FOR CHESTY COUGHS WITH CONGESTION
Use: A liquid remedy for the treatment of coughs, containing guaiphenesin, an expectorant and pseudoephedrine, a decongestant.
Dose: Adults should take 10 ml four times a day. Children (2-12 years) should be given 2.5-5 ml, according to age. Read the label for the correct dosage. This treatment is not recommended for children under two years.

ROBITUSSIN NIGHT TIME
Use: A liquid sugar-free remedy for relieving coughs, containing brompheniramine, an antihistamine, pseudoephedrine, a decongestant, and codeine, a cough suppressant.
Dose: Adults should take 5-10 ml four times a day. Children (4-12 years), should be given 5-7.5 ml three times a day, according to age. Read the label for the correct dosage. This treatment is not recommended for children under four years.

RYNACROM ALLERGY
Use: A nasal spray for relieving hayfever symptoms, containing sodium cromoglycate, an anti-inflammatory and xylometszoline, a decongestant.
Dose: One spray should be directed into each nostril four times a day. This treatment is not recommended for children under five years.

SALACTOL WART PAINT
Use: A paint for the treatment of corns and calluses, containing salicylic acid.
Dose: The product should be applied to the affected area daily and rubbed down with an emery board.

SALONAIR
Use: A spray for easing muscular aches and pains, containing rubefacients and a salicylate, an aspirin derivative.
Dose: The spray should be applied to the affected area once or twice

a day. This treatment is not recommended for children under six years.

SALONPAS PLASTERS
Use: A plaster treatment for relieving muscular aches and pains. The plasters contain rubefacients and a salicylate, an aspirin derivative.
Dose: Plaster can be replaced up to three times a day for up to seven days. Not suitable for children under 12 years.

SAVLON ANTISEPTIC CREAM
Use: An antiseptic cream for the treatment of minor wounds and irritations of the skin, containing cetrimide and chlorohexidine gluconate.
Dose: The cream should be applied to the affected part as needed.

SAVLON ANTISEPTIC WOUND WASH
Use: A liquid spray antiseptic for the treatment of minor wounds and skin irritations, containing chlorohexidine gluconate.
Dose: The product should be sprayed onto the wound in order to help wash away any dirt.

SAVLON CONCENTRATED ANTISEPTIC
Use: A liquid antiseptic containing gluconate and cetrimide for the treatment of minor wounds and skin irritations.
Dose: The product should be diluted with water as appropriate for its use.

SAVLON DRY ANTISEPTIC
Use: An antiseptic aerosol powder in the form of a spray for the treatment of minor wounds and skin irritations. The spray contains povidone iodine.
Dose: A light dusting of the powder should be sprayed onto the affected part.

SCHOLL ANTISEPTIC FOOT BALM
Use: A foot balm for relieving sore feet, containing the antiseptic menthyl salicylate, and menthol.
Dose: The product should be applied to the affected area morning and evening, or as required.

SCHOLL ATHLETE'S FOOT CREAM
Use: A cream for the treatment of athlete's foot, containing tolnaftate, an antifungal ingredient.
Dose: The product should be applied twice a day to the affected area, and for a further two weeks after the infection has cleared.

SCHOLL CORN AND CALLUS REMOVAL LIQUID

Use: A liquid for the removal of corns and calluses.
Dose: The liquid should be applied to the affected area twice a day, for no longer than two weeks. This treatment is not recommended for children under 16 years.

SCHOLL CORN REMOVAL PADS

Use: Medicated pads for the removal of corns, containing salicylic acid.
Dose: A pad should be applied once a day to the affected area until the corn can be removed. This treatment is not recommended for children under 16 years. The product is also available as Scholl Soft Corn Removal Pads.

SCHOLL CORN REMOVAL PLASTERS

Use: Medicated plasters for the removal of corns, containing salicylic acid.
Dose: The medicated plasters should be applied to the affected area once a day until the corn can be removed. This treatment is not recommended for children under 16 years. Waterproof plasters also available.

SCHOLL POLYMER GEL CORN REMOVERS

Use: A gel for the treatment of corns and calluses, containing salicylic acid.
Dose: A new plaster should be applied each day to the affected area until the corn can be removed. This treatment is not recommended for children under 16 years.

SCHOLL SEAL AND HEAL VERRUCA REMOVAL GEL

Use: A liquid treatment for the removal of verrucae, containing salicylic acid.
Dose: 1-2 drops should be applied onto the affected area once a day and allowed to dry. The treatment should be applied daily until the verruca can be removed. This treatment is not recommended for children under 12 years.

SCHOLL VERRUCA REMOVAL SYSTEM

Use: Medicated plasters for the treatment of verrucae, containing salicylic acid.
Dose: An appropriately sized plaster should be applied to the verruca and left in position for 48 hours before repeating the treatment. The treatment may be continued for up to 12 weeks if necessary. This treatment is not recommended for children under six years unless advised otherwise by a doctor.

SCR
Use: An antiseptic cream treatment for cradle cap.
Dose: The cream should be applied sparingly onto the baby's head. Massage in gently, leave for 30 minutes and then rinse off. Leave for 2 minutes on babies under a year old. A second treatment can be applied seven days later if required. Do not apply to broken or inflamed skin.

SEA-LEGS
Use: Tablets for preventing travel sickness, containing meclozine, an antihistamine.
Dose: Adults should take two tablets one hour before a journey, or on the previous evening. Children over two years should be given half to one tablet, depending on age. Read the label for the correct dosage. This treatment is not recommended for children under two years.

SECADERM
Use: A salve for the treatment of boils and other minor skin infections. It contains an analgesic and an antiseptic.
Dose: The product should be applied to the boil or skin infection and covered with a clean, dry dressing, once or twice a day.

SECRON
Use: A liquid remedy for relieving colds and flu in children, containing ephedrine, a decongestant, and ipecacuanha, an expectorant.
Dose: Children over two years should be given 2.5-10 ml 2-3 times a day, according to age. Read the label for the correct dosage. This treatment is not recommended for children under two years.

SELSUN
Use: A liquid containing selenium sulphide for the treatment of dandruff.
Dose: The liquid should be applied twice a week for two weeks, then once a week for two weeks, until the dandruff has cleared. This treatment is not recommended for children under five years.

SENOKOT TABLETS
Use: Tablets for relieving constipation, containing senna, a stimulant laxative.
Dose: Two tablets should be taken on retiring. This treatment is not recommended for children under 12 years. The product is also available in granular and liquid forms.

SETLERS ANTACID TABLETS
Use: Antacid tablets for relieving indigestion.

Dose: 1-2 tablets should be sucked or chewed as required. Take a maximum of eight tablets in 24 hours. This treatment is not recommended for children under 12 years. The product is available in several different flavours.

SINUTAB TABLETS
Use: Tablets for relieving the symptoms of colds, flu and sinusitis. Each tablet contains paracetamol and phenylpropanolamine, a decongestant.
Dose: Adults should take two tablets three times a day. Take a maximum of six tablets in 24 hours. Children (6-12 years) should be given one tablet three times a day, with a maximum of three tablets in 24 hours. This treatment is not recommended for children under six years.

SIOPEL
Use: A cream for the treatment of nappy rash, containing dimethicone, a soothing barrier cream, and cetrimide, an antiseptic.
Dose: The cream should be applied 3-5 times a day to baby's bottom, after washing and drying. Repeat this for 3-4 days and then reduce the applications to 1-2 times a day.

SOLARCAINE CREAM
Use: A cream for the treatment of bites, stings, minor burns, scalds and sunburn, containing a mild anaesthetic.
Dose: The product should be applied to the affected area 3-4 times a day. This treatment is not recommended for children under three years. The product is also available in lotion and spray forms.

SOLPADEINE CAPSULES
Use: Analgesic capsules for general pain relief, containing 500 mg of paracetamol, 8 mg of codeine phosphate and 30 mg of caffeine.
Dose: Two capsules should be taken up to two times a day. Take a maximum of eight capsules in 24 hours. This treatment is not recommended for children under 12 years.

SOLPADEINE TABLETS
Use: Analgesic tablets for general pain relief, containing 500 mg of paracetamol, 8 mg of codeine phosphate, caffeine.
Dose: Two tablets should be taken up to four times a day if required. Take a maximum of eight tablets in 24 hours. This treatment is not recommended for children under 12 years. The product is also available in soluble form.

SOLPAFLEX

Use: Analgesic tablets for general pain relief, containing 200 mg of ibuprofen and 12.8 mg of codeine phosphate hemihydrate.

Dose: 1-2 tablets should be taken every 4-6 hours as required. Take a maximum of six tablets in 24 hours. This treatment is not recommended for children under 12 years.

SOLPAFLEX GEL

Use: This is a gel for the treatment of muscular aches and pains, containing ketoprofen, a non-steroidal anti-inflammatory (NSAID).

Dose: The gel should be massaged into the affected area 2-4 times a day. This treatment is not recommended for children under 15 years.

SOMINEX

Use: Tablets for insomnia, containing promethazine, an antihistamine.

Dose: One tablet should be taken at bedtime. This treatment is not recommended for children under 16 years.

SOOTHAKE

Use: A gel to relieve toothache in adults. Gel contains chlorbutol and clove oil.

Dose: For relief only. Do not use continuously. Consult dentist as soon as possible.

SOOTHAKE TOOTHACHE TINCTURE

Use: For the relief of toothache. Pale straw coloured liquid with clovelike taste and odour containing clove oil and lignocaine.

Dose: Place cottonbud (supplied) soaked in tincture to dental cavity until pain eases. Flammable. Consult dentist if pain persists.

SOOTHELIP

Use: A cream treatment for cold sores, containing aciclovir, an antiviral.

Dose: The cream should be applied as soon as the tingling of a cold sore is felt, and then every four hours, five times a day for five days. Repeat for a further five days if necessary.

STINGOSE

Use: A pump spray for relieving the discomfort of bites and stings, containing aluminium sulphate, a soothing ingredient.

Dose: The spray should be applied liberally to the affected area, as required. This treatment is not recommended for children under three years.

STREPSILS DIRECT ACTION SPRAY

Use: A spray for sore throats, containing lidocaine, an anaesthetic.
Dose: The spray should be directed into the back of the throat three times, every three hours as required. Take a maximum of six doses in 24 hours. This treatment is not recommended for children under 12 years.

STREPSILS DUAL ACTION LOZENGES

Use: Lozenges for sore throats, containing lidocaine, an anaesthetic, and amylmetacresol and dichlorobenzyl alcohol, both antibacterials.
Dose: One lozenge should be dissolved in the mouth every two hours. Take a maximum of eight tablets in 24 hours. This treatment is not recommended for children under 12 years.

STREPSILS ORIGINAL

Use: Lozenges for relieving sore throats, containing dichlorobenzyl alcohol and amylmetacresol, both antibacterials.
Dose: One lozenge should be dissolved in the mouth every 2-3 hours. Sugar-free and vitamin C versions are also available.

STURGERON TABLETS

Use: Tablets for the prevention of travel sickness, containing cinnarazine, an antihistamine.
Dose: Adults should take two tablets two hours before the journey, followed by one tablet every eight hours if required. Children (5-12 years) should be given half the adult dose. This product is not suitable for children under five years.

SUDAFED COLD AND FLU TABLETS

Use: Tablets for easing the symptoms of colds and flu, containing paracetamol and pseudoephedrine, a decongestant.
Dose: Adults should take one tablet every 4-6 hours. Take a maximum of four tablets in 24 hours. Children (6-12 years) should be given half a tablet every 4-6 hours, with a maximum of four doses in 24 hours. This treatment is not recommended for children under six years.

SUDAFED EXPECTORANT

Use: A liquid remedy for the treatment of coughs, containing guaiphenesin, an expectorant and pseudoephedrine, a decongestant.
Dose: Adults should take 10 ml four times a day. Children (6-12 years) should be given 5 ml. Children (2-5 years) should be given 2.5 ml. This treatment is not recommended for children under two years.

SUDAFED LINCTUS

Use: A liquid remedy for coughs, containing dextromethorphan, a cough suppressant, and pseudoephedrine, a decongestant.

Dose: Adults should take 10 ml four times a day. Children (6-12 years) should be given 5 ml. Children (2-5 years) should be given 2.5 ml. This treatment is not recommended for children under two years.

SUDAFED NASAL SPRAY

Use: A spray for easing nasal congestion caused by colds. The spray contains oxymetazoline, a decongestant.

Dose: 1-2 sprays should be directed into each nostril twice or three times a day. This treatment is not recommended for children under six years. Do not use for more than a week.

SUDAFED TABLETS

Use: Tablets for relieving cold and flu symptoms, containing pseudoephedrine, a decongestant.

Dose: One tablet should be taken every 4-6 hours. Take a maximum of four tablets in 24 hours. This treatment is not recommended for children under 12 years.

SUDOCREAM

Use: A cream for the treatment of nappy rash, containing zinc oxide, an antiseptic and astringent, and hypoallergenic lanolin.

Dose: The cream should be applied thinly to baby's bottom as required.

SULEO M LOTION

Use: A lotion for the treatment of lice and scabies, containing malathion and alcohol.

Dose: The lotion should be applied to dry hair and rubbed in well. The hair should be allowed to dry naturally, washed out after 12 hours and then combed through while still wet. This treatment is not recommended for babies under six months.

SWARM

Use: A cream for the treatment of bites and stings, containing witch hazel and an anti-microbial.

Dose: The product should be applied to the affected area as required.

SYNDOL

Use: Analgesic tablets for general pain relief, containing 450 mg of paracetamol, 10 mg of codeine phosphate, 30 mg of caffeine, and doxylamine succinate, an antihistamine.

Dose: 1-2 tablets should be taken every 4-6 hours as required. Take a maximum of eight in 24 hours. This treatment is not recommended for children under 12 years.

SYNTARIS HAYFEVER

Use: A nasal spray for relieving the symptoms of hayfever, containing flunisolide, a corticosteroid.

Dose: Adults should take two sprays into each nostril morning and evening, with a maximum of four sprays for each nostril in 24 hours. For children (12-16 years) direct one spray into each nostril up to three times a day, with a maximum of three sprays per nostril in 24 hours. This treatment is not recommended for children under 12 years.

TAGAMET 100

Use: Tablets for relieving indigestion, heartburn and general gastric discomfort. They contain cimetidine, a histamine H2 antagonist which reduces the production of stomach acid.

Dose: Two tablets should be taken when symptoms arise. For indigestion at night, one tablet should be taken one hour before retiring. Take a maximum of eight tablets in 24 hours. This treatment is not recommended for children under 16 years. Do not use for longer than two weeks. The product is also available in a liquid form.

TANCOLIN

Use: A liquid remedy for the treatment of coughs, containing dextromethorphan, a suppressant, and vitamin C.

Dose: Children (6 months -12 years) should be given 2.5-15 ml, three times a day according to age. Read the label for the correct dosage. This treatment is not recommended for babies under six months.

TAVEGIL

Use: Tablets for the relief of allergic rhinitis, including hayfever, allergic dermatoses, urticaria, angioneurotic oedema and drug allergy. White tablets each contain clemastine hydrogen fumarate.

Dose: Adults and children over 12 years should take 1-3 tablets. Children (6-12 years) should take half to one tablet. 3-6 years should take half a tablet. Children (1-3 years) should take a quarter to half a tablet. Dose to be taken night and morning. May cause drowsiness.

TCP ANTISEPTIC OINTMENT

Use: An antiseptic ointment for the treatment of minor wounds and skin irritations, containing iodine, methyl salicylate, salicylic acid, sulphur, tannic acid, camphor and TCP liquid antiseptic.

Dose: The product should be applied to the affected area as required.

TCP FIRST AID ANTISEPTIC CREAM

Use: An antiseptic cream for the treatment of minor wounds and irritations of the skin. It contains chloroxylenol, triclosan, sodium salicylate and TCP liquid antiseptic.

Dose: The product should be applied to the affected area as required.

TCP LIQUID

Use: A liquid antiseptic for the treatment of minor wounds and irritations of the skin, containing phenol and halogenated phenols.
Dose: The liquid should be diluted according to use, or applied undiluted to spots and mouth ulcers.

TCP SORE THROAT LOZENGES

Use: Lozenges for easing sore throats, containing antibacterial phenols.
Dose: One pastille should be sucked or chewed as required. This treatment is not recommended for children under six years.

TEARS NATURALE

Use: Artificial tear and lubricant for relief of dry eyes. Colourless, sterile solution containing a duasorb water soluble polymeric system, dextran and hypromellose.
Dose: One or two drops as frequently as necessary to relieve eye irritation symptoms. Not for use with soft contact lenses.

T-GEL

Use: A medicated shampoo for the treatment of dandruff, containing coal tar.
Dose: The product should be massaged into wet hair and scalp and then rinsed. Repeat once or twice a week.

TIGER BALM RED (REGULAR AND EXTRA STRENGTH)

Use: An ointment for easing muscle pain, containing various rubefacients.
Dose: The balm should be rubbed gently into the affected area 2-3 times a day. This treatment is not recommended for children under two years.

TINADERM CREAM

Use: An antifungal cream for the treatment of athlete's foot, containing tolnaftate.
Dose: The cream should be applied twice a day to the affected area.

TINADERM POWDER PLUS

Use: This is a powder treatment for athlete's foot, containing tolnaftate, an antifungal ingredient.
Dose: The powder should be sprinkled over the infected area and into socks and footwear, twice a day. The product is also available in spray form.

TIXYLIX CATARRH SYRUP

Use: This is a syrup for the treatment of catarrh, containing diphenhydramine, an antihistamine and menthol.

Dose: Children (6-10 years) should be given 10 ml four times a day. Children (1-5 years) should be given 5 ml four times a day.

TIXYLIX CHESTY COUGH
Use: A liquid remedy for relieving coughs, containing guaiphenesin, an expectorant.
Dose: Children should be given 2.5-10 ml according to age. Read the label for the correct dosage. This treatment is not recommended for babies under one year.

TIXYLIX DAYTIME
Use: A liquid remedy for the treatment of coughs, containing pholcodine, a cough suppressant.
Dose: Children should be given 2.5-10 ml every six hours, according to age. Read the label for the correct dosage. This treatment is not recommended for babies under one year. A night-time version is also available, containing promethazine, an antihistamine.

TIXYLIX INHALANT
Use: Capsules for relieving cold and flu symptoms in children. Each capsule contains menthol, eucalyptus oil, camphor and turpentine oil.
Dose: For babies (3-12 months), the capsule should be cut and its contents squeezed onto a handkerchief tied out of reach, so that the vapours can be inhaled. For children one year and over, the contents should be sprinkled over bed linen or night clothes. Alternatively the capsule can be emptied into a bowl of hot water and left out of reach but close enough for the vapours to be inhaled.

TOEPEDO
Use: This is a cream treatment for athlete's foot, containing keratolytics.
Dose: The cream should be applied sparingly to the affected area twice daily until the infection has cleared.

TOPAL
Use: Tablets for easing general digestive discomfort, containing an antacid and an alginate.
Dose: 1-3 tablets should be taken four times a day after meals and on retiring. This treatment is not recommended for children under 12 years.

TORBETOL
Use: A lotion for the treatment of acne and spots, containing cetrimide and chlorhexidine, both anti-microbials.
Dose: The lotion should be applied to the affected area up to three times a day. This treatment is not recommended for children under 15 years.

TRAMIL

Use: Analgesic capsules for general pain relief, containing 500 mg of paracetamol.

Dose: Two capsules should be taken every four hours as required. Take a maximum of eight in 24 hours. This treatment is not recommended for children under 12 years.

TRANSVASIN HEAT RUB

Use: A cream for easing muscular aches and pains, containing rubefacients and a salicylate, an aspirin derivative.

Dose: The cream should be applied to the affected area up to three times a day. This treatment is not recommended for children under six years.

TRANSVASIN HEAT SPRAY

Use: A spray for the treatment of various muscular aches and pains, containing rubefacients and a salicylate, an aspirin derivative.

Dose: The product should be sprayed onto the affected area up to three times a day. This treatment is not recommended for children under five years.

TRAXAM PAIN RELIEF GEL

Use: A gel for relieving muscular aches and pains, containing felbinac, a non-steroidal anti-inflammatory (NSAID).

Dose: The gel should be rubbed into the affected area 2-4 times a day. This treatment is not recommended for children under 12 years.

TROSYL DERMAL CREAM

Use: A cream for the treatment of athlete's foot, containing tioconazole, an antifungal ingredient.

Dose: The product should be applied to the affected area once or twice a day.

TUMS

Use: Antacid tablets for relieving indigestion and heartburn.

Dose: 1-2 tablets should be taken as required. Take a maximum of 16 tablets in 24 hours. This treatment is not recommended for children under 12 years.

TYROZETS

Use: Lozenges for relieving sore throats, containing tyrothricin, an antibacterial and benzocaine, an anaesthetic.

Dose: One lozenge should be dissolved in the mouth every three hours. Take a maximum of eight in 24 hours. Children (3-11 years) should be given a maximum of six lozenges in 24 hours. This treatment is not recommended for children under three years.

ULTRABASE
Use: An emollient cream for the relief of eczema and dermatitis, containing a mixture of oils.
Dose: The product should be applied as required.

ULTRAMOL
Use: An analgesic tablet for the relief of most painful and febrile conditions. Contains paracetamol, codeine and caffeine.
Dose: Adults and children over 12 years should take one or two tablets dissolved in water every 4-6 hours up to four times a day. Not more than 8 tablets in any 24 hour period. Not recommended for children under 12 years. Use with care in severe renal or hepatic impairment.

UNGUENTUM MERCK
Use: An emollient cream for relieving the discomfort of eczema, dermatitis and nappy rash, containing a mixture of various oils.
Dose: The cream should be applied as required.

UNIFLU WITH GREGOVITE C TABLETS
Use: Tablets for the relief of flu, colds, nasal and sinus congestion, sneezing, coughing, runny nose, headaches, fever, aching limbs, and nasal congestion in allergic conditions such as hay fever. Uniflu tablets contain paracetamol, codeine phosphate, phenylephrine hydrochloride, caffeine and diphenhydramine hydrochloride. Gregovite C contains ascorbic acid.
Dose: Adults should take one of each tablet every six hours until the symptons disappear. Maximum of four Uniflu tablets in 24 hours. Children over 12 should take one of each tablet. Maximum of three Uniflu tablets in 24 hours. Do not use during pregnancy.

UNIGEST
Use: Antacid tablets for relieving indigestion, heartburn and general digestive discomfort.
Dose: 1-2 tablets should be sucked or chewed after meals and at bedtime. This treatment is not recommended for children under 12 years.

VALPEDA
Use: A cream for the treatment of common foot ailments such as athlete's foot and cracked or scaly skin. Cream contains halquinol.
Dose: Rub over feet and between toes night and morning, preferably after bathing feet in warm water.

VAGISIL MEDICATED CREAM

Use: Cream for the relief of vaginal and rectal itching, thrush itching. Contains lignocaine.

Dose: Apply liberally 3-4 times a day. For external use only. Not for use on extensive body areas. If symptoms persist for more than a week, discontinue use and consult a doctor. Not suitable for children under 12 years. Do not use in pregnancy without first consulting a doctor.

VASOGEN CREAM

Use: A cream for the treatment of nappy rash, containing zinc oxide, an antiseptic and astringent, and calamine, a soothing ingredient.

Dose: The product should be applied to baby's bottom after washing and drying.

VEGANIN

Use: Analgesic tablets for general pain relief containing 250 mg of paracetamol, 250 mg of aspirin and 6.8 mg of codeine phosphate.

Dose: 1-2 tablets should be taken every three to four hours as required. Take a maximum of eight tablets in 24 hours. This treatment is not recommended for children under 12 years.

VENO'S DRY COUGH

Use: A liquid remedy for the treatment of coughs, containing glucose and treacle.

Dose: Adults should take 10 ml every two to three hours. Children (3-12 years) should be given 5 ml. This treatment is not recommended for children under three years.

VENO'S EXPECTORANT

Use: A liquid remedy for the treatment of coughs, containing guaiphenesin, an expectorant, glucose and treacle.

Dose: Adults should take 10 ml every two to three hours. Children (3-12 years) should be given 5 ml every 2-3 hours. This treatment is not recommended for children under three years.

VENO'S HONEY AND LEMON

Use: A liquid remedy for the treatment of coughs, containing lemon, glucose and treacle.

Dose: Adults should take 10 ml every 2-3 hours. Children (3-12 years) should be given 5 ml. This treatment is not recommended for children under three years.

VERACUR

Use: A gel for the treatment of verrucae and warts, containing formaldehyde.

Dose: Apply twice a day.

VERRUGON
Use: An ointment remedy for the treatment of verrucae, containing salicylic acid.
Dose: The felt ring should be placed on the verruca, and the ointment applied and covered with a plaster. This should be repeated daily. This treatment is not recommended for children under six years.

VESAGEX
Use: An antiseptic white cream for cuts, abrasions, minor burns, minor skin disorders, dry and cracked skin and nappy rash. Contains cetrimide.
Dose: Apply as required.

VICKS MEDINITE
Use: A liquid remedy for relieving coughs, containing dextromethorphan, a cough suppressant, ephedrine, a decongestant, doxylamine, an antihistamine and paracetamol.
Dose: Adults should take 30 ml on retiring. Children (10-12 years) should be given 15 ml. This treatment is not recommended for children under 10 years.

VICKS ORIGINAL COUGH SYRUP (CHESTY COUGH)
Use: A liquid remedy for the treatment of coughs, containing guaiphenesin and sodium citrate, both expectorants and cetylp yearidium, an antiseptic.
Dose: Adults should take 10 ml every three hours if required. Children (6-12 years) should be given 5 ml. This treatment is not recommended for children under six years.

VICKS SINEX DECONGESTANT NASAL SPRAY
Use: A nasal spray for clearing the congestion caused by colds, flu and sinusitis. It contains oxymetazoline, a decongestant.
Dose: 1-2 sprays should be directed into each nostril every six to eight hours. This treatment is not recommended for children under six years. Do not use for longer than seven days.

VICKS ULTRA CHLORASEPTIC
Use: A throat spray for relieving sore throats, containing benzocaine, an anaesthetic.
Dose: Adults should take three sprays every 2-3 hours. Children (6-12 years) should be given one spray every 2-3 hours. Take a maximum of eight doses in 24 hours. This treatment is not recommended for children under six years, and should not be used for more than three consecutive days.

VICKS VAPORUB

Use: An inhalant rub for easing congestion caused by colds and flu, containing menthol, eucalyptus and camphor.

Dose: A small amount should be rubbed into the chest, throat and back at night. Alternatively, two teaspoons can be added to a bowl of hot water and the vapours inhaled. This treatment is not recommended for babies under six months.

VICKS VAPOSYRUP FOR CHESTY COUGHS

Use: A liquid remedy for relieving coughs, containing guaiphenesin, an expectorant.

Dose: Adults should take 15 ml up to six times a day. Children (6-11 years) should be given 10 ml. Children (2-5 years) should be given 5 ml. This treatment is not recommended for children under two years.

VICKS VAPOSYRUP FOR DRY COUGHS

Use: A liquid remedy for coughs, containing dextromethorphan, a cough suppressant.

Dose: Adults should take 15 ml up to four times a day. Children (6-11 years) should be given 5 ml. Children (2-5 years) should be given 2.5 ml. This treatment is not recommended for children under four years.

VICKS VAPOSYRUP FOR TICKLY COUGHS

Use: A liquid remedy for the treatment of coughs, containing menthol.

Dose: Adults should take 10 ml every 3-4 hours. Take a maximum of six doses in 24 hours. Children (6-12 years) should be given half the adult dose. This treatment is not recommended for children under six years.

VIRASORB

Use: A cream treatment for cold sores, containing aciclovir, an antiviral.

Dose: The cream should be applied as soon as a cold sore tingling is felt, and then every four hours, five times a day for five days. Repeat for a further five days if necessary.

VITATHONE

Use: An ointment for the treatment of chilblains. It contains menthyl nicotinate, which helps to relieve the itchiness by stimulating the circulation.

Dose: The ointment should be applied every 2-3 hours as required. This treatment is not recommended for children.

VOCALZONE

Use: Pastilles for easing sore throats.

Dose: One pastille should be dissolved in the mouth as needed, every two hours if necessary. This treatment is not recommended for children under 12 years.

WARTEX OINTMENT

Use: An ointment for the removal of warts, containing salicylic acid.
Dose: The product should be applied to the wart daily until the wart can be removed. This treatment is not recommended for children under six years.

WASP-EZE OINTMENT

Use: An ointment for the treatment of bites and stings, containing an antihistamine.
Dose: The product should be applied to the affected area immediately and then every hour if necessary, for up to 24 hours. This treatment is not recommended for children under one year. The product is also available as a spray.

WAXSOL EAR DROPS

Use: Ear drops for removing earwax, containing softening ingredients.
Dose: The ears should be filled with the liquid for two consecutive nights before syringe treatment.

WAX WANE EAR DROPS

Use: Ear drops for the removal of earwax, containing softening ingredients.
Dose: 4-5 drops should be directed into the ear and plugged with cotton wool. This should be repeated 2-3 times a day for several days or until the wax softens.

WITCH DOCTOR GEL

Use: An astringent gel for the treatment of bites, stings, minor burns, scalds, sunburn and bruises, containing witch hazel.
Dose: The product should be applied to the area as required. The product is also available as a stick.

WOODWARD'S BABY CHEST RUB

Use: An inhalant rub for easing congestion caused by colds and flu. It contains menthol, eucalyptus and turpentine.
Dose: A small amount should be rubbed onto the chest, throat and back so that the vapours can be inhaled during the night. This treatment is not recommended for babies under three months.

WOODWARD'S COLIC DROPS

Use: A liquid remedy for relieving infant colic and wind, containing dimethicone, an anti-wind ingredient. A measure is supplied.

Dose: For children under two years, one measured dose of 3 ml should be given before each feed.

WOODWARD'S GRIPE WATER
Use: A liquid remedy for relieving infant colic and wind, containing sodium bicarbonate, an antacid and dill oil.
Dose: 5-10 ml (according to age) should be given after or during feeds. Check the label for the correct dosage. Give a maximum of six doses in 24 hours. This treatment is not recommended for babies under one month.

WOODWARD'S NAPPY RASH OINTMENT
Use: An ointment for the treatment of nappy rash, containing zinc oxide, an antiseptic and an astringent, and cod liver oil, a moisturiser.
Dose: The product should be applied to baby's bottom three times a day after washing and drying.

WOODWARD'S TEETHING GEL
Use: A gel for relieving teething pain in babies, containing lignocaine, an anaesthetic, and an antiseptic.
Dose: The gel should be applied and then reapplied after 20 minutes. This can be repeated every three hours if necessary.

WRIGHT'S VAPOURIZING FLUID
Use: An inhalant to be used in conjunction with Wright's Vaporizer, containing chlorocesol. It's vapours help to ease congestion caused by colds and flu.
Dose: 10 ml should be added to the vaporizer block every eight hours. This treatment is not recommended for children under two years.

YARIBA
Use: Tablets used as a pick-me-up in temporary tiredness.
Dose: Adults and children over 14 years should take one or two tablets three times a day. Not to be taken during pregnancy or lactation.

YEAST-VITE
Use: A tablet remedy for alleviating fatigue, containing caffeine, vitamin B1 and nicontamide.
Dose: Two tablets should be taken every 3-4 hours as required. Take a maximum of 12 tablets in 24 hours. This treatment is not recommended for children.

YESTAMIN PLUS TABLETS
Use: A tablet remedy for relieving fatigue, containing caffeine, yeast and glucose.
Dose: Two tablets should be taken three times a day. This treatment

is not recommended for children.

VISCOTEARS LIQUID GEL
Use: Liquid gel tear substitute containing carbomer for the relief of dry eye conditions including keratoconjunctivitis sicca; also for unstable tear film.
Dose: Adults should take one drop three or four times daily, or as required. Contact lenses should not be worn during administration. Not for use by children unless advised by a doctor.

ZANTAC 75 TABLETS
Use: Tablets for easing digestive discomfort, containing rantidine, a histamine H2 antagonist which helps to reduce the production of stomach acid.
Dose: One tablet should be taken initially, followed by one more if necessary. Take a maximum of four tablets in 24 hours. This treatment is not recommended for children under 16 years. Do not use for more than two weeks.

ZENOXONE
Use: White cream for the relief of mild to moderate eczema, irritant contact dermatitis, allergic contact dermatitis and insect bite reactions. Cream contains hydrocortisone.
Dose: Apply sparingly over a small area once or twice daily for a maximum of 7 days. For external use only.

ZIRTEK
Use: A tablet for relieving the symptoms of hayfever, containing cetirizine, an antihistamine.
Dose: One tablet should be taken each day. This treatment is not recommended for children under 12 years.

ZIZ
Use: Tablets to relieve temporary sleep problems. Contain promethazine hydrochloride.
Dose: Two tablets at bedtime. May be taken up to an hour before going to bed. The elderly should take one tablet initially which may be increased to two. Not recommended for children under 16 years. Do not take if driving or operating machinery. Alcohol to be avoided. If suffering from glaucoma, consult your doctor.

ZIZ FORTE
Use: Tablets to relieve temporary sleeplessness. Contain promethazine hydrochloride.
Dose: One tablet at night about one hour before going to bed when there is difficulty in falling asleep. Do not take more than two tablets

in 24 hours. Do not take if driving or operating machinery. Alchohol to be avoided. If suffering from glaucoma, consult the doctor.

ZOVIRAX COLD SORE CREAM
Use: A cream treatment for cold sores containing aciclovir, an antiviral.
Dose: The cream should be applied as soon as the tingling of a developing cold sore is felt. Continue to apply every four hours, five times a day for up to ten days.